'n thin thick 'n thin thick 'n thin thick 'n thin thick 'n thin thick 'n thin thick 'n thin thick 'n thin thick 'n thin thick 'n
n thin thick 'n thin thick 'n thin thick 'n thin thick 'n thin thick 'n thin thick 'n thin thick 'n thin thick 'n thin thick 'n
ck 'n thin thick 'n thin thick 'n thin thick 'n thin thick 'n thin thick 'n thin thick 'n thin thick 'n thin thick 'n thin thic
thick 'n thin thick 'n thin thick 'n thin thick 'n thin thick 'n thin thick 'n thin thick 'n thin thick 'n thin thick 'n thin

The best of

Weaver's

23 Designers

32 Projects

18 Comprehensive articles

from

18 years of

Prairie Wool Companion

and

Weaver's Magazine

THICK'nTHIN

PUBLISHER
Alexis Yiorgos Xenakis

EDITOR
Madelyn van der Hoogt

PUBLISHING DIRECTOR
David Xenakis

GRAPHIC DESIGNER
Bob Natz

PHOTOGRAPHER
Alexis Yiorgos Xenakis

PRODUCTION DIRECTOR
Denny Pearson

BOOK PRODUCTION MANAGER
Carol Skallerud

DIGITAL COLOR SPECIALIST
Jason Bitner

PRODUCTION ARTISTS
Jay Reeve
Everett Baker
Natalie Sorenson

SECOND PRINTING, 2005; FIRST PUBLISHED IN USA IN 2001
BY XRX, INC., PO BOX 1525, SIOUX FALLS, SD 57101-1525

ISBN 1-893762-08-4

Produced in Sioux Falls, South Dakota, by XRX, Inc., 605.338.2450

Printed in USA

 BOOKS

'n thin thick 'n thin

The best of
Weaver's

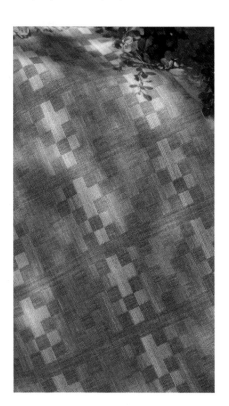

THICK'nTHIN

 BOOKS

Authors &

Contents

thick 'n thin thick 'n thin

introduction

Weaver's editor Madelyn van der Hoogt gathers together in this volume the ground-breaking collection of articles on thick 'n thin weaves that appeared in *Weaver's* magazine over the last decade. During that time, *Weaver's* became a venue that belies conventional wisdom that there is nothing new in weaving. Under Madelyn's leadership, *Weaver's* grew to be a treasured resource for the designer/weaver, and with a stupendous team of contributors, she brought *Weaver's* readers something new, issue after issue.

Madelyn followed David Xenakis as editor of *Prairie Wool Companion* in 1986 and was editor of *Weaver's* from 1988-1999.

In the last decade, handweavers have enjoyed an explosive period of discovery—in fibers, structures, color interaction, finishing techniques, tools, and more. Each new discovery has followed so rapidly on the heels of others, that readers barely had time to digest the content of each new issue of *Weaver's* before another one appeared at the door. Gathered in this single volume are scattered jewels that clearly belong together, and the result is a whole much greater than the sum of its parts.

In *Thick 'n Thin*—the second book in our *Best of Weaver's* series—you'll find a dazzling collection of serendipitous surprises that have come as answers to the weaver's favorite question: What if? The basic principles of a little-known structure called diversified plain weave are reworked, expanded, extended, and applied in a number of innovative ways to create patterned fabrics that are drapable, sturdy, and richly textured—on as few as two shafts.

Thick 'n Thin begins by giving basic tips for drafting and weaving these unique structures that alternate very thick and very thin fibers in both warp and weft. Diversified plain weave is only the beginning; thick 'n thin warps and wefts are used in log cabin, summer and winter, three-tie weaves, crackle, overshot, double weave, lampas, and others. Over thirty projects illustrate the principles and include a wide range of fabric types, from rugs and blankets to fine silk scarves to placemats, towels, and table linens. You'll learn how to prepare the warp and thread the loom with challenging fiber combinations, how to create your own effective designs, how to use these weaves with profile drafts—every aspect is thoroughly explained.

You can use this book as a source for great projects. You can use it to learn color and design principles. You can use it to gain a new understanding of how threads interact. When you've mastered the basic principles, you can use it to ask your own What ifs. Whatever you choose to use it for, you will turn to *Thick 'n Thin* again and again.

Madelyn

thick 'n thin thick 'n thin thick 'n thin thick 'n thin thick 'n thin thick 'n thin thick 'n thin thick 'n thin thick 'n thin thick 'n
thin thick 'n thin thick 'n thin thick 'n thin thick 'n thin thick 'n thin thick 'n thin thick 'n thin thick 'n thin thick 'n thin thick 'n
thin thick 'n thin thick 'n thin thick 'n thin thick 'n thin thick 'n thin thick 'n thin thick 'n thin thick 'n thin thick 'n thin thick

diversified plain weave family

Here are complete steps for warping back to front or front to back with special fibers. Use them for thick 'n thin drafts—and for other projects that present warping challenges.

WARPING TIPS

There are two basic ways to warp a loom: 'back to front' or 'front to back'. Most of us learn one way and use it exclusively—whether or not it is the most effective way for the materials, setts, loom geometry, or space we're working in—simply because we are used to doing it that way. (Sectional warping, which requires special equipment, is not described here.)

The names we use for the two ways are in themselves a little misleading since the warp winds on the beam in the same direction in both. They should really be called 'beaming before threading' or 'threading before beaming.'

There are advantages to both. A wise weaver learns how to use both and chooses the most appropriate one for each specific warp and loom.

Beam before threading if
❏ the materials are sticky, overtwisted, dense, or fragile,
❏ it is most comfortable to sit in front of your loom for threading.

The usual order of steps to follow with this method is:
❏ wind the warp,
❏ spread the warp in a raddle,
❏ wind the warp on the warp beam,
❏ suspend lease sticks behind the shafts and, sitting in front of the shafts, thread the heddles,
❏ sley the reed,
❏ tie the warp onto the front apron rod.

Thread before beaming if
❏ the yarns are relatively smooth and strong,
❏ it is most comfortable to sit behind the shafts for threading,
❏ you wish to design warp color sequences in the reed.

The usual order of steps to follow with this method is:
❏ wind the warp,
❏ sley the reed,
❏ sitting behind the shafts, thread from the reed (or suspend lease sticks between the reed and the shafts and thread from the lease sticks),
❏ wind the warp on the warp beam,
❏ tie the warp onto the front apron rod.

Back to front (beaming before threading)

In the weave structures in this volume, very thin and very thick threads alternate in the warp. During beaming, the very thin threads, especially if they are stiff, wiry, slightly overspun, and/or of a different fiber than the thicks, have a strong tendency to twist and tangle with the softer, loftier thick threads.

The usual argument for beaming before threading is to avoid wear and tear on the warp, minimize friction, and prevent the tangling that can occur when the warp threads have to separate from each other to pass through the heddles during beaming in the front-to-back method. The usual back-to-front method, however, includes placing a pair of lease sticks in the cross and winding the entire warp onto the warp beam with the lease sticks in place. Threads that pass through a one-and-one cross to get to the warp beam experience as much wear and tear (if not more) and are as likely to tangle (if not more likely) as when passing through heddles. It only makes sense to choose back to front for difficult fibers if lease sticks are not used in the process.

To do this, you will need a raddle with a finer spacing than one dent/inch. The finer the number of raddle dents/inch the better. Construct a 4-dent/inch raddle by hammering finishing nails into a scrap board. Stagger the nails so as not to crack the board. Before winding the warp, calculate the number of ends in ¼" (i.e., 6/dent for 24 epi in a 4-dent raddle).

❏ Wind the thick and thin warps together. For most of the drafts in this volume, this means holding one thick and one thin end separated by the index finger (if the draft calls for 2 thin/1 thick, wind all three together, keeping all three separate with the fingers). Allow the two (or three) ends to pass through the threading cross together. At the opposite end from the threading cross (usually at the bottom of the warping board), make a second 'raddle' cross. Place the number of threads in this cross that will be sleyed in each dent of the raddle, six ends in our example.

❏ Secure the raddle and threading crosses with ties. Tie a very firm choke tie about 25" from the raddle cross. Cut both ends of the warp and remove the warp from the warping board (chain from the threading cross to the raddle cross).

❏ With the raddle secured to the back beam, spread the warp in the raddle using the raddle cross. (Allow the other end of the warp chain to rest in front of the loom on a clean sheet spread out on the floor.) The easiest way to do this is to put

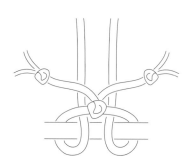

1. A square knot ties the warp onto front and back apron rods.

the second and fourth fingers of your left hand through the loops on both sides of the cross and your middle finger behind it. Remove the ties that secured the cross. Pull each group of threads from the cross with your right hand and place each group in a raddle dent. As you go, secure the tops of the finishing nails with rubber bands to keep the threads from jumping out of the raddle.

❏ When the warp is completely spread and secured in the raddle, tie the warp onto the back apron rod as in *1* (it may be necessary to pull the warp through the raddle dents a distance; the choke will prevent misalignment). Cut the choke tie. At the front of the loom separate the warp into 2–3" sections and slide your finger between them down to the floor; maintain this separation during the entire beaming process. Wind the warp onto the back beam with paper or narrow sticks as spacers. After each turn, return to the front of the loom and pull very firmly on the 2–3" groups of warp threads. (Note that no lease sticks are used, the raddle alone spreads and directs the order of the threads. It won't matter if they do not go on the beam in perfect order; tension during weaving will align them. Since the warp only meets the smooth, spaced nails of the raddle, very little impedes its swift progress onto the beam.) It is important to tighten the 2–3" groups evenly as you go, or the threading cross will not present itself evenly at the opposite end. Take turns tightening in different orders, from the left, from the right, from the center. Pull as tightly as you can without breaking the fine threads. (I usually wrap each section of threads around a smooth stick and pull on the stick to save abrading my hands with the fibers.)

'n thin thick 'n thin thick 'n thin thick 'n thin thick 'n thin thick 'n thin thick 'n thin thick 'n thin thick 'n thin thick 'n thin thick 'n thin thick 'n thin t
'n thin thick 'n thin thick 'n thin thick 'n thin thick 'n thin thick 'n thin thick 'n thin thick 'n thin thick 'n thin thick 'n thin thick 'n thin thick 'n thin t
k 'n thin, thick 'n thin thick 'n thin thick 'n thin thick 'n thin thick 'n thin thick 'n thin thick 'n thin thick 'n thin thick 'n thin thick
thick 'n thin thick 'n thin thick 'n thin thick 'n thin thick 'n thin thick 'n thin thick 'n thin thick 'n thin thick 'n thin thick 'n thin t

der Hoogt Madelyn van der Hoogt Madelyn van der Hoogt Madelyn van der Hoogt Madelyn van der

- When you have reached the end of the warp at the front of the loom, insert lease sticks in the threading cross and suspend them behind the shafts. Cut the ties that secure the cross, and working from one side to the other, pull groups of warp threads downward so that the threads come straight and smooth from the back beam to form a clear cross at the lease sticks. Trim the warp to an even length (unwind or wind the beam if necessary), long enough to pass through the heddles (plus about 12") for threading. Thread the heddles.
- Sley the reed.
- Tie onto the front apron rod as in *1*.

Front to back (threading before beaming)

Although beaming before threading may be the most trouble-free method when you are working with thick 'n thin fibers, you may prefer threading first. Here are front-to-back steps to use with thick 'n thin warps.

- Wind one warp of the thick ends and a separate warp of the thin ends with a threading cross at one end of each warp. Tie one very tight choke in each warp chain at a distance from the cross appropriate for securing the warp to the breast beam for threading (20–30" from the cross ends). I use doubled carpet warp and a surgeon's knot (wrap the right tail around the left tail twice for the first half of a square knot; don't tie the second half of the square knot yet). Tie the cross to secure. Cut the bottom ends of the warp; chain the warp up to reach the top right peg; hang the chain from the peg; tighten the half choke tie as firmly as possible and then tie the second half of a square knot (left over right); cut the ends of the warp at the top peg; remove the warp chain from the board.
- Place the reed on a table in a position comfortable for sleying (propped with heavy books or in reed holders). Holding the cross in your left hand, with your right hand slip the hook through each successive dent and grab each thread or pair of threads and pull through the dent. (If you're new at this, pull each thread off the cross and free it from the rest of the warp with your fingers and then sley.) Sley the thick ends as instructed by the draft (for these projects, this will usually be 1/dent in a 10-dent or 12-dent reed or 2/dent in an 8-dent reed). The cross can be abandoned as each end is sleyed. Tie a cord to the reed above the thick ends (tie it around each side-bar of the reed so that the reed is divided into two sections, an upper and a lower section). You can use a stick for this purpose, but

it is easier to see which dent each end is in if only a cord separates the two warps. Sley the thin ends above the thick ends (again, abandon the cross as the threads are sleyed).

- Take the reed and warps to the loom and place the reed in the beater; allow the warp chains to rest on a clean sheet on the floor. Tie the chokes to the center of the breast beam. (No thread should *ever* be allowed to slip in the chokes.) Sometimes it helps to raise or brace a loom so that it slants up toward you for better access. Take the extra time to provide good light for threading and a comfortable position for you. If you have used a rod to separate the two warps, secure the rod in the middle of the reed so that you can see the thick ends below the rod and the thin ends above the rod clearly from your threading position behind the shafts. Thread the heddles. For some of the drafts you will thread a thin/thick pair from one dent followed by a thick/thin pair from the next dent. Be sure that you always thread warp ends next to each other that come from the same dent. When you have ½" threaded, tie an overhand knot in the ends (they will be even without adjusting when pulled gently against their secured position at the choke tie on the breast beam). Proceed until the threading is completed.
- Then tie the knotted ½" groups around the back apron rod as in *1*. There will be no tension on these ends; simply tie them all so that their tails are about the same length. There is no need to remove the overhand knots at the ends of the bouts. You may have to cut the chokes to have enough length to make this tie.
- If you haven't already done so, at the front of the loom, untie or cut the chokes and determine that the two warps are still separate and not twisted around each other. (At this point, if you discover that some ends are twisted, it is easier to correct them after the warp is beamed, though the beaming process will be a little slower in order to guide the twisted ends through the heddles.) Pull firmly on both warps to straighten. Never comb! Remove the rod or cord at the reed. Holding the two warps tightly with one hand so that both warps are under considerable tension, with the other hand strum any areas that appear tangled. Gently divide the combined warp into 2–3" sections at the front beam; slide your fingers down the divisions to the chains on the floor (maintain these separations throughout beaming). Wind the warp onto the

back beam with paper or narrow sticks as spacers. After each turn, return to the front of the loom and pull very firmly on the 2–3" warp sections. I usually wrap each section of warp several times around a smooth stick and pull on the stick. If any threads are twisted or loose, adjust only the errant threads; do not comb or realign any others.

- Tie onto the front apron rod as in *1*. If the warp is narrow, free the apron rod cords on the sides so that the rod does not bend. Tie in small groups, ½" warp width for each knot. Tie the first half of a square knot for all the groups across the warp. Then, working from the center out, pull the tails of the first half firmly but not tightly, then tie the second half of each. If you pull the tails too tight for this knot, each succeeding knot will become a little tighter aided by the support of the preceding knots. Say "firm not tight" as you tie each one.)

THIN FIBER TIPS

If you use sewing thread for the thin threads, choose a good-quality all-cotton sewing or quilting thread for best results. Cotton-covered polyester has a tendency to tangle. Rayon sewing thread is difficult to tie on (it is very slippery; knots may require glue), although it almost never tangles. Place the spool on the spindle of a shuttle or on a rod so that the thread unwinds as the spool rotates. Pulling the thread off the end of the spool adds twist, which can cause an even greater tendency to tangle. If your thin warp threads are a dark color (or blue or gray) they may be difficult to see. Place a piece of white paper under the loom when threading and under the reed when sleying.

TWISTED FRINGES

Many of the throws, scarves, and shawls in this volume are finished with a twisted fringe. Calculate the number of ends desired for each fringe so that they divide evenly into the total number of warp ends. Choose a number that coincides with color orders or breaks in the weave structure as well as considering desired fringe bulk.

Divide the number of threads for one fringe into two groups. Holding one in each hand, twist both groups in one direction firmly, until they begin to kink. Then hold them in one hand and twist them together in the opposite direction; secure the ends with an overhand knot. Several manufacturers offer fringe twisters. One advantage to using a twister is that the number of twists can be counted and exactly the same number used for each fringe. ✄

Madelyn van der Hoogt Madelyn van der Hoogt Madelyn van der Hoogt **Madelyn van der Hoogt** Madely.

'Diversified plain weave' is a term coined by Klara Cherepov in her 1972 monograph by the same name. Ever since, the structure has enchanted—and frustrated—handweavers. Thick and thin threads in both warp and weft produce a deliciously drapable textured and patterned fabric.

The frustration results from more than its awkward name! Diversified plain weave is also awkward to thread and weave. Moreover, each pattern block hungrily consumes two shafts (in addition to shafts 1 and 2) when DPW is used with profile drafts.

Diversified plain weave

A draft for diversified plain weave on six shafts is shown in *1a*. Since the usual draft format does not show the relative sizes of warp and weft threads, the draft is rewritten using representative symbols in *1b*. The drawdown in *1b* shows the appearance of a cloth in which the thick warp is dark, the thin warp and weft are light, and the thick weft is a medium value.

Notice that each thick warp thread nestles between a pair of thin warp threads, and each thick weft thread nestles between a pair of thin weft threads (white in this draft). These thin threads form a small square frame around the thick warp thread (if it is raised for the thick pick) or the thick weft thread (if the thick warp thread is down). For the first thick pick in *1b*, for example, the thick warp thread on shaft 3 is framed by the thin threads, but the thick weft is framed where warp threads are down on shafts 4, 5, and 6.

Threading and treadling units

Klara Cherepov's version of diversified plain weave requires that even shafts and odd shafts alternate throughout the threading. Therefore, a thick thread on an odd 'pattern' shaft appears between thin threads on shaft 2; and, alternately, a thick thread on an even 'pattern' shaft appears between thin threads on shaft 1. In the treadling, a thick pick (with shaft 1 and selected thick warp threads raised) appears between two thin picks of the even tabby, and alternately, a thick pick (with shaft 2 and selected thick warp threads raised) appears between two thin picks of the odd tabby.

If the thick threads were all removed, a basketweave fabric of thin threads would remain. If the thin threads were all removed, only thick floats of various sizes would remain (and no viable fabric). Diversified plain weave is actually a basket weave fabric of thin threads on which a thick supplementary warp *and* a thick supplementary weft are tied down in a regular order by the thin threads to show on either the face or the back of the cloth to form pattern or background.

1a. Diversified plain weave draft

If blocks are not repeated in the threading and treadling, six shafts produce four blocks and one pattern treadle is required for each block combination.

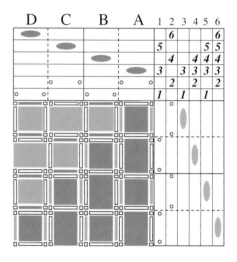

1b. DPW draft with drawdown

1c. DPW draft with blocks repeated in threading and treadling

If blocks are repeated in the threading and treadling, six shafts produce only two blocks and two pattern treadles are required for each block combination.

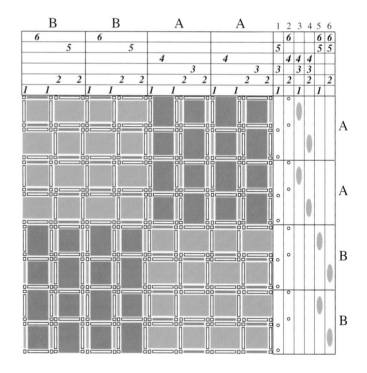

DPW drawbacks

The weaving process for diversified plain weave is somewhat awkward. A shuttle with the thin weft weaves a pick of even tabby, traveling, say, from left to right. The thick weft is inserted next (left to right, say) with shaft 1 and selected thick warp threads raised. The shuttle with the thin weft then returns

'n thin thick 'n thin thick 'n thin thick 'n thin thick 'n thin thick 'n thin thick 'n thin thick 'n thin thick 'n thin thick 'n thin thick 'n thin thick 'n thin thick 'n thin thick 'n thin thick 'n thin thick 'n thin thick 'n thin thick 'n thin thick 'n

der Hoogt *Madelyn van der Hoogt* Madelyn van der Hoogt *Madelyn van der Hoogt* Madelyn van der Hoogt **Madelyn van der H**

(right to left) in the same tabby shed as for the first pick. For the fourth pick it travels in the opposite tabby shed as the first pick but from the same side of the loom (left to right)—the position of the shuttle provides no clue as to which tabby sequence is next. The thick weft then returns (now right to left), but with shaft 2 and selected thick warp threads raised.

Weavers are often willing to put up with awkward treadling sequences if the results are striking, either in pattern, texture, or color interaction. True DPW, however, has some design limitations.

Diversified plain weave threadings must observe the threading order: 2 EP 2, 1 OP 1 (EP = thick thread on even pattern shaft; OP = thick thread on odd). When blocks are threaded in alternating, straight, or point order, each pattern shaft can provide an independent block of pattern. Six shafts produce the 4-block design in *1b*, for example. If a profile draft is used in which blocks are repeated in the threading, however, each block requires two pattern shafts. If Block A is threaded for more than one profile threading square, for example, 2-3-2-1-4-1 must be repeated for the required width (2-5-2-1-6-1 for Block B, etc.; see *1c*). In this case, eight shafts provide only three blocks and four shafts only one.

A new draft for DPW

Weaving mythology tells us that many of the weaves we love are the result of serendipitous mistakes. The structure in *2* owes its evolution to two years of workshops in 'Thick 'n Thin' and the creative students who discovered solutions to the unweavable drafts devised by their teacher in an effort to get more pattern blocks from fewer shafts. Frances Schultz's treadling solution for one experimental draft and Lynne McCalla's inspired misreading of another combine to create a new way of threading and weaving a derivative of diversified plain weave that eliminates the major drawbacks of the original.

Advantages of the new draft

In the new draft, the structural threading unit is simply 1-2-P (P = any pattern shaft; thins are threaded on shafts 1 and 2, thicks on P). Each pattern shaft acts as an independent block, and blocks can be repeated as desired; see *2a-c*. Four shafts produce two independent blocks; eight shafts produce six.

The treadling sequence is also simplified in this version. Two thin picks, 1–2 vs all the pattern shafts

2a. The new draft

Six shafts produce four blocks no matter what the threading order of the pattern shafts and one treadle is required for each block combination.

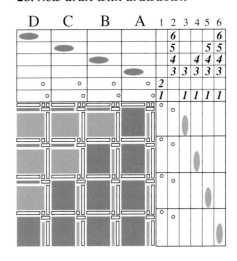

2b. New draft with drawdown

2c. New draft with blocks repeated in threading and treadling

Four units of Block A and four units of Block B are threaded.

The thick warp makes pattern in Block A for four treadling units and in Block B for four treadling units.

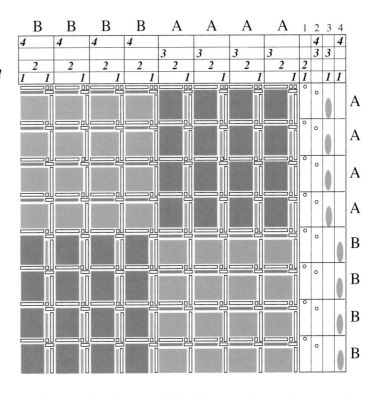

(i.e., 3 through the number available), are followed by the thick pick in which shaft 1 is raised with selected thick warp threads. The shuttle with the thin thread enters the 1–2 shed from one side, the 3–n shed from the other; shuttle order is easy to follow.

An additional advantage is that fewer treadles are required: since shaft 1 is raised for all of the pat-

tern (thick) picks, one pattern treadle instead of two is required for each different block combination.

Other differences

The cloth produced by the new draft differs structurally from original DPW in that the thin threads do not form a basket weave ground cloth. In fact, if the

thick 'n thin thick 'n thin thick 'n thin thick 'n thin thick 'n thin thick 'n thin thick 'n thin thick 'n thin thick 'n thin thick '
k 'n thin thick 'n thin thick 'n thin thick 'n thin thick 'n thin thick 'n thin thick 'n thin thick 'n thin thick 'n thin thick 'n thin thick
thin thick 'n thin thick 'n thin thick 'n thin thick 'n thin thick 'n thin thick & thin thick 'n thin thick 'n thin thick 'n thin thick 'n th
k 'n thin thick 'n thin thick 'n thin thick 'n thin thick 'n thin thick 'n thin thick 'n thin thick 'n thin thick 'n thin thick 'n thin thick
k 'n thin thick 'n thin thick 'n thin thick 'n thin thick 'n thin thick 'n thin thick 'n thin thick 'n thin thick 'n thin thick 'n thin thick

thick threads were removed from the new DPW, no interlacement of the thin threads would remain. (The new version is easy to thread and weave, but not so easy to classify.)

This fact does not disturb the structural stability of the cloth, though a slight difference in visual surface texture is related to it. A close examination of the drawdown in *1b*, p. 8, shows that the alternate rectangles that represent the thick warp and weft threads are slightly different in size; that is, a larger rectangle alternates with a slightly smaller rectangle in each direction. In the drawdown produced by the new draft in *2b*, however, all rectangles are the same size; compare also *Photos a* and *b*, p. 11. The alternating smaller/larger bumps that appear in the original DPW add a slight textural emphasis to the surface of the fabric.

Color choices

An important contribution to the appearance of fabrics produced by both drafts is the relative values and hues selected for the thick and thin threads in both warp and weft. The drawdowns in *1b* and *2b* show a dark thick warp, a light thin warp, a medium thick weft and a light thin weft. This choice emphasizes the grid formed by the thin threads (see also *Photos c* and *d*). Very light thin threads can be the least successful color choice as they tend to wash out the colors of the thick yarns.

In *3a* and *3b* the thick and thin warp threads are dark, and the thick and thin weft threads are light. This choice also emphasizes the grid made by the thin threads, but it appears as a dark overlay where light thicks show and as a light overlay where dark thicks show (see also *Photo e*).

In *4a* and *4b* the thick warp is the same value and hue as the thin weft, and the thick weft is the same value and hue as the thin warp. The resulting drawdown shows vertical stripes in the warp direction and horizontal stripes in the weft direction. The same effect occurs if the hues are different but the values are the same; in *Photo f*, the thick weft and thin warp are both dark, but they are different hues.

Design choices

Consider several factors when deciding which DPW draft to use. The slightly different-sized bumps produced by the original DPW emphasize the texture of

the thick yarns. Choose this drafting method if you like this effect and you are willing to sacrifice pattern blocks and treadling ease to achieve it.

Twill and overshot patterns can be easily adapted to both forms of DPW. Since their threadings usually alternate even shafts with odd shafts, they can be used without loss of pattern capacity with the original DPW system if desired. Simply rewrite the twill or overshot draft on shafts 3 and beyond. Place the twill or overshot tie-up in the pattern section of the diversified plain weave tie-up. A rosepath twill becomes a design for diversified plain weave in *5a*.

With block profile drafts, use the new system. To thread following a profile threading draft, substitute one 3-thread unit for every square in the profile threading: A = 1-2-3, B = 1-2-4, C = 1-2-5, D = 1-2-6, etc.; see *5b*. If a larger-scale design is desired, simply multiply the number of times each thick thread (with its preceding thins on 1-2) is threaded.

Practice weaving original diversified plain weave with projects by Ruth Morrison (who also wove the fabrics in *Photos a–f*), Mary Schneider, and Alice Schlein. Try the new version with projects by Marina O'Connor and Tracy Kaestner. ✄

3a. Original DPW:
black thick and thin warp
gray thick and thin weft

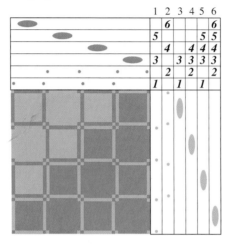

3b. New DPW:
black thick and thin warp
gray thick and thin weft

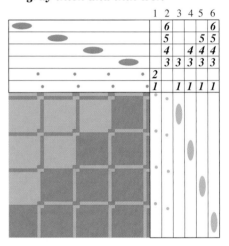

4a. Original DPW:
black thick, gray thin warp
gray thick, black thin weft

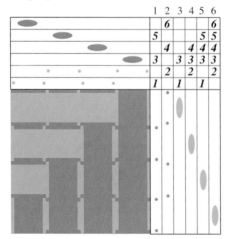

4b. New DPW:
black thick, gray thin warp
gray thick, black thin weft

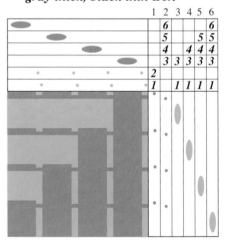

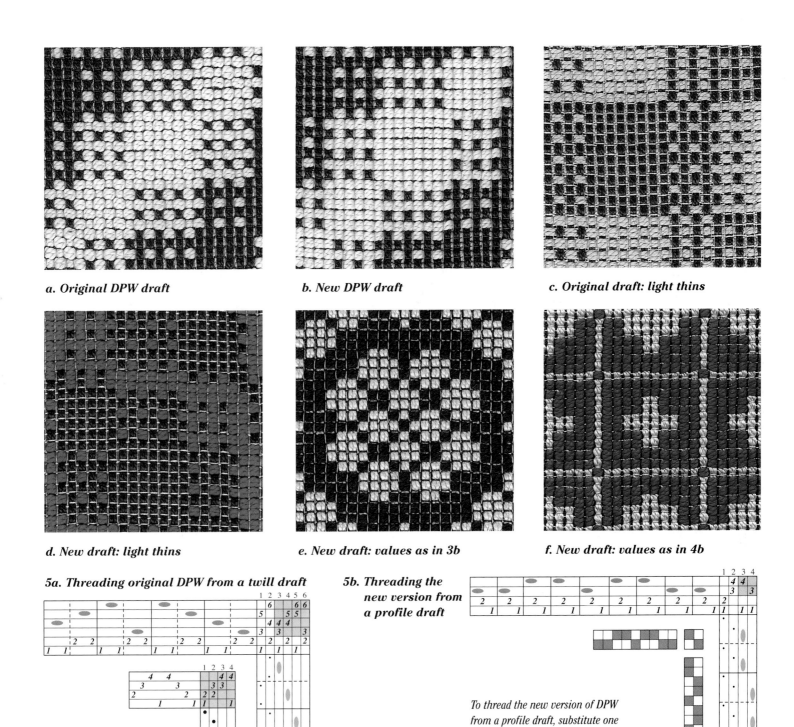

a. Original DPW draft

b. New DPW draft

c. Original draft: light thins

d. New draft: light thins

e. New draft: values as in 3b

f. New draft: values as in 4b

5a. Threading original DPW from a twill draft

To use a twill draft for the pattern threading of DPW, rewrite the twill threading on shaft 3 and beyond. Only use original DPW (if desired) when the twill draft alternates odd and even shafts throughout.

5b. Threading the new version from a profile draft

To thread the new version of DPW from a profile draft, substitute one 3-thread unit (or more) for each square in the profile threading draft. Substitute one 3-pick treadling sequence for each square in the profile treadling draft. (Twill drafts can be used with the new version of DPW following the same method as for the original version; see **5a**.)

thick 'n thin scarf and jacket

Ruth Morrison Ruth Morrison Ruth Morrison *Ruth Morrison* Ruth Morrison **Ruth Morrison** *Ruth Morris*

The fabrics for the bomber jacket and scarf are both woven from a true diversified plain weave draft (see pp. 8–11). The lofty, soft silk used for the thick threads in both the warp and weft is especially suitable for a thick 'n thin weave, adding to its luxurious drapability. The special nature of the weave structure also reveals the full beauty of the rich colors in the space-dyed threads.

❏ Equipment. 8-shaft loom (or 4-shaft loom for a checked design; checks are ¾" square), 36" weaving width for jacket, 8" for scarf; 4 dent/inch raddle (see pp. 6–7); 8-dent reed; 2 shuttles.

❏ Materials. Thick warp: soft-spun 2-ply silk (800 yds/lb, Lambspun of Colorado, PO Box 320, Ft Collins, CO 80524), Purple Majesty, 2 lb for jacket, 2½ oz for scarf. Thick weft: soft-spun 2-ply silk, natural, 1⅛ lb for jacket, 2 oz for scarf. Thin warp and weft: 50/3 cotton or cotton sewing thread, natural, 6000 yds for jacket, 200 yds for scarf; Vogue pattern #1226 or similar, lining, notions required by pattern.

❏ Wind a warp for jacket of 288 thick and 576 thin ends 5½ yds long; for scarf wind 44 thick and 88 thin ends 2½ yds long. Hold 1 thick/2 thin ends together in the hand; keep separate with fingers. Prepare a threading cross at one end (3 ends in each group) and a raddle cross at the other (6 ends in each group).

❏ Spread raddle cross in raddle at 36" width for jacket, 5½" for scarf; beam without lease sticks as described on pp. 6-7. The warp will be positioned on the back beam by the raddle.

❏ Place lease sticks in the threading cross and thread following the draft in *1*, *2*, or *3*.

❏ Sley 1 thick and 2 surrounding thins in each dent of an 8-dent reed, 24 total epi; jacket fabric width is 36"; scarf width is 5½".

❏ Weave following the treadling in *1*, *2*, or *3*.

❏ Finish by securing edges with machine zigzagging or 2 rows of straight stitching. Soak in washing machine, warm water; agitate a few seconds; add vinegar to rinse. Repeat soak; add fabric softener to rinse. Lay over smooth rod to dry; press.

❏ Cut out pattern pieces for jacket; zigzag raw edges, and sew together one at a time to ensure matching of diagonal fabric design. Construct jacket according to pattern directions. For scarf, prepare twisted fringe of two thicks and four thins in each fringe. ✂

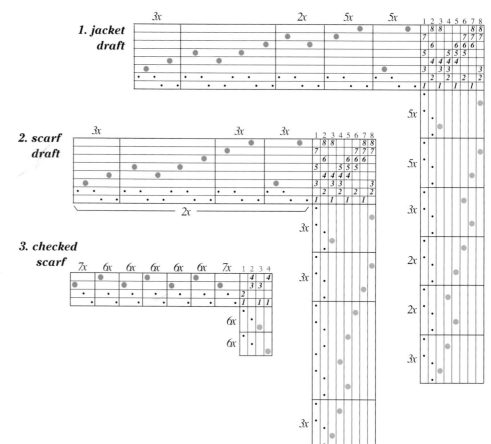

1. jacket draft

2. scarf draft

3. checked scarf

thick 'n thin thick 'n t

Ruth Morrison Ruth Morrison Ruth Morrison Ruth Morrison Ruth Morrison Ruth Morrison Ruth Morrison Ruth Morrison Ruth Morriso

Since the very fine weft in this structure allows the thick warp colors to show without dilution, space-dyed or ikat yarns are particularly successful. On four shafts, show all thick warp on one side, all thick weft on the other.

A soft-spun silk is used for the thick threads in this jacket. Experiment with various wools, silk or rayon chenilles, soft cottons, or multiple strands of other fibers for equally successful garment-weight fabrics.

overshot patterning in diversified plain weave

Overshot patterns without long floats? Who wouldn't love a block weave with the rich diversity of 4-shaft overshot that is not limited by practical float length! Diversified plain weave can produce a 4-block design that looks like overshot but has no floats—on only six shafts.

Ten shafts are required for four independent blocks of diversified plain weave (see pp. 8–11). The 6-shaft draft in *1*, however, also provides four blocks, but because adjacent blocks share shafts, the halftones occur like those we usually associate with overshot. In the same way as in overshot, the halftones are produced in two opposite blocks (B and D, for example) when a third block (A, for example) weaves solid pattern and its opposite (C, for example) solid background.

In the draft in *1*, light-colored thick warp ends are threaded on shafts 3–6, and very thin warp ends are threaded on shafts 1 and 2 (these can be a dark, light, or neutral color; see pp. 10–11 for a discussion of the effects of color choices for the thin warp and weft threads).

The threading of the thick ends determines the pattern blocks: Block A = 3, 4; B = 4, 5; C = 5, 6; D = 6, 3. Each thick end on an *even* pattern shaft is threaded between two thin ends on *shaft 1*; each thick end on an *odd* pattern shaft is threaded between two thin ends on *shaft 2*. Note that each block shares a shaft with the two blocks that are adjacent to it.

The tie-up and treadling sequence in *1* shows thin tabby picks surrounding each dark thick pick. Note that the *even* tabby precedes and follows pattern treadles that raise *shaft 1* with selected pattern shafts and the *odd* tabby precedes and follows pattern treadles that raise *shaft 2* with selected pattern shafts. When a pattern (thick) pick is made, either the dark thick weft shows on the face of the cloth (in blocks where thick warp ends are *not* raised) or the light thick warp shows on the face (in blocks where thick warp ends *are* raised). The tie-up in *1* produces pattern (dark) in Block A with treadles 3 and 4, in B with treadles 5 and 6, in C with treadles 7 and 8, and in D with treadles 9 and 10.

However, when pattern shafts 3 and 4 are down to show the dark thick weft in Block A, the dark weft also covers *one* of the light thick warp threads in Block B and *one* of the light thick warp threads in Block D. Blocks B and D therefore produce halftones; see the dark, light, and halftone blocks in the mat, p. 17.

1. Diversified plain weave: four blocks with halftones

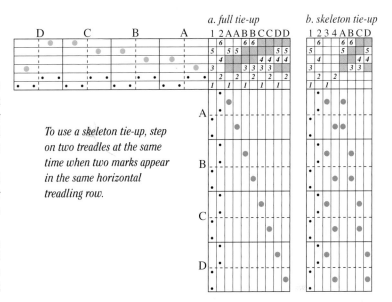

To use a skeleton tie-up, step on two treadles at the same time when two marks appear in the same horizontal treadling row.

Because 6- and 8-shaft looms are usually limited to eight or ten treadles, a skeleton tie-up (*1b*) provides the required number of sheds. For each thick pick, two treadles are used, one with shaft 1 (tr 3) and one with shaft 2 (tr 4).

To thread a 4-block diversified plain weave draft in an overshot pattern, first write out a complete overshot draft as in *2a* (used for the mat, adapted from 'Winter's Rest,' *Keep Me Warm One Night*, Dorothy and Harold Burnham, and 'Sorrel Blossom,' *Shuttle-Craft Book of American Hand-Weaving*, Mary Atwater).

Transfer the overshot threading exactly as it is from shafts 1–4 to shafts 3–6; this becomes the threading for the thick warp ends; see *2b*. Before and after each thick end on an even shaft, place a thin warp end on shaft 1, and before and after each thick end on an odd shaft, place a thin warp end on shaft 2.

2a. Overshot threading draft

2b. Part of the overshot threading draft transposed to diversified plain weave

ck 'n thin thick 'n thin thick 'n thin thick 'n thin thick 'n thin thick 'n thin thick 'n thin thick 'n thin thick 'n thin thick 'n thin thick 'n thin thick
ck 'n thin thick 'n thin thick 'n thin thick 'n thin thick 'n thin thick 'n thin thick 'n thin thick 'n thin thick 'n thin thick 'n thin thick 'n thin thick
thin thick 'n thin thick 'n thin thick 'n thin thick 'n thin thick 'n thin thick 'n thin thick & thin thick 'n thin thick 'n thin thick 'n thin thick 'n t
ck 'n thin thick 'n thin thick 'n thin thick 'n thin thick 'n thin thick 'n thin thick 'n thin thick 'n thin thick 'n thin thick 'n thin thick 'n thin thick
ck 'n thin thick 'n thin thick 'n thin thick 'n thin thick 'n thin thick 'n thin thick 'n thin thick 'n thin thick 'n thin thick 'n thin thick 'n thin thick

3a. Blocks are circled in the overshot draft

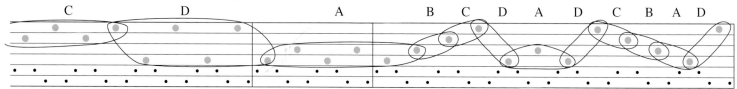

3b. Blocks are circled in the diversified plain weave draft

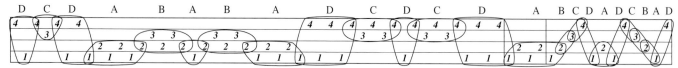

Weaving the blocks

There are two basic ways to weave these drafts (in addition to varying block size and order to create different designs). The first is a slight modification of treadling 'as-drawn-in.' Notice how the treadles are numbered in *4a*. Read the threading draft in *3b* and substitute the treadle number for the shaft number in the threading using corresponding thick and thin threads. In addition to the pattern treadle, however, also step on the treadle that raises the thin warp threads that were not raised in the preceding tabby shed. For example, for the first 3-pick sequence, the threading draft reads 1-6-1. Use these treadles, but also raise shaft 2 with treadle 6. The treadling for part of the threading in *3b* using this method is shown in *4a*.

The second method produces more closely the appearance of overshot. Blocks must first be identified in the threading. The two shafts that compose each block are circled in *3a* and *3b*. Examine the tie-up in *4b*. Each pattern treadle is identified with a block letter. For each block circled in the threading, use the pattern treadle that is assigned to that block. For the first 3-pick sequence, for example, use tabby treadle 1 for the thin picks and pattern treadle D with shaft 2 for the thick pick. For the next 3-pick sequence, use tabby treadle 2 for the thin picks and pattern treadle A with shaft 1 for the thick pick. (Note that the thin warp threads that are not raised in the preceding tabby shed are always raised with the pattern treadle for the thick pick.) For each circled block, use 1 pattern (thick) pick fewer than the number of thick warp ends in the circle. The treadling for part of the threading in *3b* is shown in *4b*. (With this method there will be one more 3-pick sequence in a complete woven piece than with *4a*.) ✂

4a. By threads

4b. By blocks

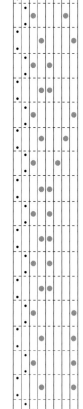

Read the threading draft to find the treadle number for the thick pick. Weave tabby with treadle 1 before and after a thick pick with shaft 2, and tabby with treadle 2 before and after a thick pick with shaft 1.

From treadling method 4a

From treadling method 4b

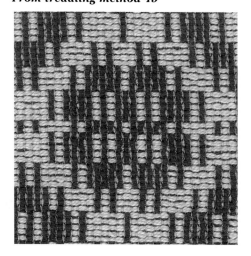

'n thin thick 'n thin thick 'n thin thick 'n thin thick 'n thin thick 'n thin thick 'n thin thick 'n thin thick 'n thin thick 'n thin thick 'r
thin thick 'n thin thick 'n thin thick 'n thin thick 'n thin thick 'n thin thick 'n thin thick 'n thin thick 'n thin thick 'n
thick 'n thin thick 'n thin thick 'n thin thick 'n thin thick 'n thin thick 'n thin thick 'n thin thick 'n thin thick
thick 'n thin thick 'n thin thick 'n thin thick 'n thin thick 'n thin thick 'n thin thick 'n thin thick 'n thin thick 'n thin t

fleece for the 21st century

The advent of synthetic fleece has brought lots of vibrant colors and patterns to outerwear fashions. Purples, bright fuchsias, and luminous teals brighten the ski slopes while 'natural' fabrics seem to come only in 'natural' tones.

No more! Diversified plain weave offers limitless color and pattern variations, while the 100% wool felt is not only warm and cozy but is also windproof as well as fireproof—unlike the 'meltable' synthetics.

1. Draft for vest

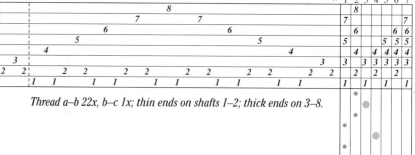

Thread a–b 22x, b–c 1x; thin ends on shafts 1–2; thick ends on 3–8.

JOANIE'S VEST

For our Alaskan winters I want my handwoven outerwear to be not only warm and colorful, but durable, too. Fabric for outdoor activities should not snag, stretch, pill, or fray. Felting this thick 'n thin structure creates an amazingly stable, sturdy fabric. You'll know what I mean when you experience your first cut into a soft, lofty handwoven fabric that does not ravel!

☐ Equipment. 8-shaft loom, 37" weaving width; 12-dent reed; 1 boat shuttle for thin weft; 4 ski shuttles for thick weft (or more if using more weft colors).

☐ Materials. In both warp and weft use 100% wool (not super-wash wool; it will not felt). If you're not sure of the fiber content of a yarn, test it by burning: If it smells like hair burning and is self-extinguishing, it is wool. If it melts into a black goo, it is synthetic. The thick threads should be five or six times the diameter of the thin threads. Although they show very little after felting, thin threads in lighter, brighter analogous colors add a jewel-like quality.
Thin warp: 20/2 100% worsted wool (5600 yds/lb, Webs), light teal, ¼ lb (worsted wool has the strength to be used as a warp). Thick warp: 8/4 100% wool (1120 yds/lb, Webs) or 4-ply Germantown worsted (1000 yds/lb, Halcyon), medium green and medium blue, ¾ lb total. Thin weft: 20/2 wool, light fuchsia, ¼ lb. Thick weft: 8/4 wool (or substitute other wools with a looser twist for more loft such as 3-ply rug wool), red, lavender, purple, maroon, or related hues, ½–¾ lb total; a simple vest pattern that accommodates a thick fabric; ¼ yd ultrasuede in coordinated color for edging if desired.

☐ Wind a warp of 221 thick ends 3 yds long in random green and blue stripes (stripe width for this vest varies from 5 ends to 20 ends each stripe) for one vest. Wind a warp of 442 thin ends 3 yds long. Estimate shrinkage at 30% in length and 23% in width. Roughly this means a 37" x 37" piece of fabric is reduced, after washing, to 26" length x 28½" width. Because of the possible variations in shrinkage as a result of different fibers or treatment during finishing, don't take my word for it. *Make your own samples!* These instructions should yield enough fabric for a simple vest; add to amounts for sampling.

☐ Sley 1 thick end in every other dent of a 12-dent reed, 6 epi; center for 36¾". Place a stick over the thick warp and sley 1 thin end in every dent. (There will be 2 ends in every other dent, 1 thick, 1 thin; 1 thin end in the alternate dents.)

☐ Thread following the draft in *1*, thin ends on shafts 1–2, thick ends on 3–8. Select the threads carefully so that the thin ends do not twist around the thick ends; make sure the thin end and the thick end in the dents that have 2 ends are threaded adjacent to each other.

☐ Beam both warps on the same beam.

☐ Weave following the treadling sequence in *1* to produce diamonds. Vary the pattern by making smaller diamonds or repeating one, two, or three blocks for small squares and stripes. Once you start you'll find it easy to create designs at the loom. Repeating narrow blocks in small vertical stripes on one side results in the opposite color predominating on the other side. No need to worry about selvedges since you'll be cutting the fabric into pattern pieces, but a beautiful fringe can be made by leaving 1–2" lengths of the heavy weft hanging out on one or both sides.

☐ Finish by removing from loom; stitch raw edges. Hold your breath and put the fabric in the washing machine on large load setting (giving it plenty of room to move) hot wash/cold rinse, mild soap, gentle cycle. Turn every few minutes. Pull it out and see how it has been transformed! Then, take another breath, put the fabric in the dryer on normal setting. Before it is completely dry—wool dries quickly—take it out and block it. I usually use 1½" brads to nail the fabric to a board and leave it overnight or until completely dry. Remember that this process is *very* variable. Keep careful records of exact minutes and temperatures if you hope to weave your fabric again. (Compare the fabric samples for the vest, p. 19, one before finishing, the other after finishing.)

☐ Cut out pattern pieces, sew with flat-felled seams for reversibility. Bind the edges with ⅝" strips of ultrasuede or any suitable edging. If fabric does not lie flat, block again; wool is very responsive. ✄

thick 'n thin t

Waller Joanie Waller Joanie Waller Joanie Waller Joanie Waller Joanie Waller Joan Waller Joanie Waller

fabric before finishing

fabric after finishing

Forget synthetic fleece! Weave a thick, soft, and insulating fleece of 100% wool. With felted diversified plain weave, you'll get glorious, pure adjacent colors and all the design potential of six blocks on eight shafts or two blocks on four. All you need is your loom– and your washer and dryer.

network drafting through thick and thin

lice Schlein Alice Schlein Alice Schlein Alice Schlein Alice Schlein **Alice Schlein** *Alice Schlein Alice Sc*

Thread once; weave huck. Tie on a new warp, re-sley, and weave a very different structure. The same network used for developing threadings for networked huck lace (see The Best of Weaver's: Huck Lace, *pp. 58–61) can be used for diversified plain weave. Since networked drafts are time-consuming to thread, you'll appreciate this double-duty draft! (To learn more about network drafting, see* Network Drafting: An Introduction, *1994, by Alice Schlein.)*

Diversified plain weave is a term coined by the late Klara Cherepov and presented in her 1972 self-published monograph, *Diversified Plain Weave* (see also pp. 8–11 for more information about diversified plain weave). The term is misleading because the structure is not really plain weave. Thick warp threads and weft threads, usually different from each other in color, form pattern or background where one or the other appears on the face of the cloth. They are outlined by adjacent thin threads in both warp and weft that act to 'tie down' their heavier neighbors. The threading and picking sequence is always thin-thick-thin; thin-thick-thin, etc. The weave is appealing because of the patterning freedom: there is no limit to the length or width of pattern blocks!

Principles of diversified plain weave

Just as with huck lace threadings, diversified plain weave threadings always follow a 2-P-2-1-Q-1 sequence, where 'P' is threaded on any odd-numbered shaft except 1, and 'Q' is threaded on any even-numbered shaft except 2. Ends on shafts 1 and 2 are threaded throughout the warp. The minimum number of shafts required for the structure is four (see the draft in *1*), although more interesting designs can be woven on eight or more shafts.

A comparison between this threading and its rules and the threading and rules for huck make evident that any threadings that are developed for networked huck can be used for diversified plain weave. Compare the minimum component for building a diversified plain weave network on 16 shafts in *2a* with the same template that is used for 3-thread huck (*The Best of Weaver's: Huck Lace*, p. 58). Just as with huck lace, ends on shafts 1 and 2 are threaded throughout without interruption since they do not affect the pattern. Note that in the final threading, any odd shaft can be threaded between ends on shaft 2, and any even shaft between ends on shaft 1.

Diversified plain weave (16 shafts)

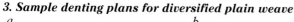

1. 4-shaft draft

a. thick warp threads show

b. thick weft threads show

2a shows the minimum component for a 16-shaft network for diversified plain weave; 2b shows a sample network. The black squares on shafts 1 and 2 are constant and represent the thin threads. Gray squares on the remaining 14 shafts indicate legal positions for the thick threads; any one may be chosen, but only one per column. Reading from the right, in every 6-end sequence, the second end is always on an odd-numbered shaft, and the fifth end is always on an even-numbered shaft. The first and third ends are always on shaft 2, and the fourth and sixth ends are always on shaft 1.

2. Sample network for diversified plain weave

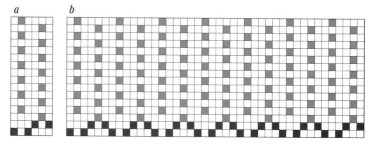

3. Sample denting plans for diversified plain weave

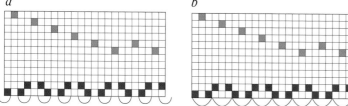
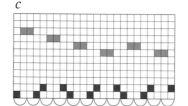
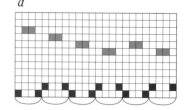

In 3a each pair of thin ends is sleyed together and each thick end is sleyed singly. In 3b each thick and two adjacent thin ends are sleyed together. In 3c (thick ends are doubled) one thick and one thin are sleyed together. In 3d two thick and the adjacent two thins are sleyed together.

thin thick 'n thin thick 'n thin thick 'n thin thick 'n thin thick 'n thin thick 'n thin thick 'n thin thick 'n thin thick 'n thin thick 'n thin thick 'r
thin thick 'n thin thick 'n thin thick 'n thin thick 'n thin thick 'n thin thick 'n thin thick 'n thin thick 'n thin thick 'n thin thick 'n thin thick 'n
thick 'n thin thick 'n thin thick 'n thin thick 'n thin thick 'n thin thick 'n thin thick 'n thin thick 'n thin thick 'n thin thick 'n thin thick 'n thin
thick 'n thin thick 'n thin thick 'n thin thick 'n thin thick 'n thin thick 'n thin thick 'n thin thick 'n thin thick 'n thin thick 'n thin thick 'n thin t

Alice Schlein Alice Schlein Alice Schlein Alice Schlein Alice Schlein Alice Schlein Alice Schlein Alice Schlein Alice Schlein Alice Sc

*Warm a winter afternoon with Alice's afghan in diversified plain weave. Though this piece is woven on
16 shafts, eight can produce a very similar design; see an alternate 8-shaft draft for the blanket on p. 24.*

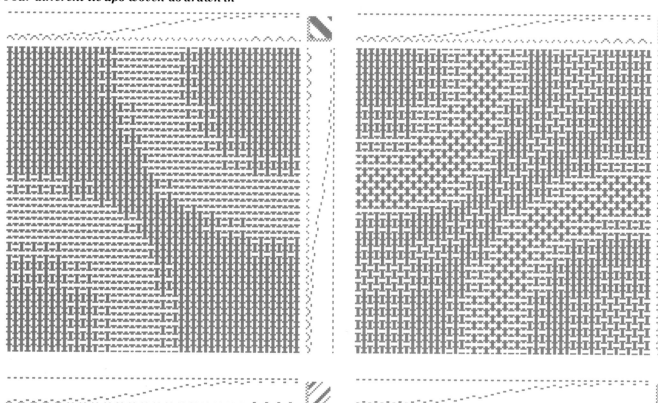

4a.

4a shows a typical tie-up for networked diversified plain weave. Treadles 1 and 2 raise alternate shafts and are used for the thin picks. The remaining treadles are used for the thick picks. When treadle 1 is used for the thin picks, a pattern treadle raising shaft 2 is used for the thick pick; when treadle 2 is used for the thin picks, a pattern treadle raising shaft 1 is used for the thick pick. The 14 x 14-square `pattern' section of the tie-up can show any arrangement, but placing a 14-shaft twill tie-up in this section produces a very effective design. 4b shows four color-and-weave drawdowns that simulate the appearance of a networked diversified plain weave threading with twill-based tie-ups treadled as-drawn-in. Thick warp threads are black (thin, white); thick wefts white (thin, black).

4b. Four different tie-ups woven as-drawn-in

thick &thin thick & thin thick & thin thick & thin thick & thin thick & thin thick & thin thick & thin thick & thin thick & thin thick & thin thick & thin thick A& thi
hin thick &thin thick & thin thick & thin thick & thin thick & thin thick & thin thick & thin thick & thin thick & thin thick & thin thick & thin
& thin thick &thin thick & thin thick & thin thick & thin thick & thin thick & thin thick & thin thick & thin thick & thin thick & thin thick & th
ick &thin thick & thin thick & thin thick & thin thick & thin thick & thin thick & thin thick & thin thick & thin thick & thin thick & thin thick & thin thick & t

5. Two sequences in threading and treadling

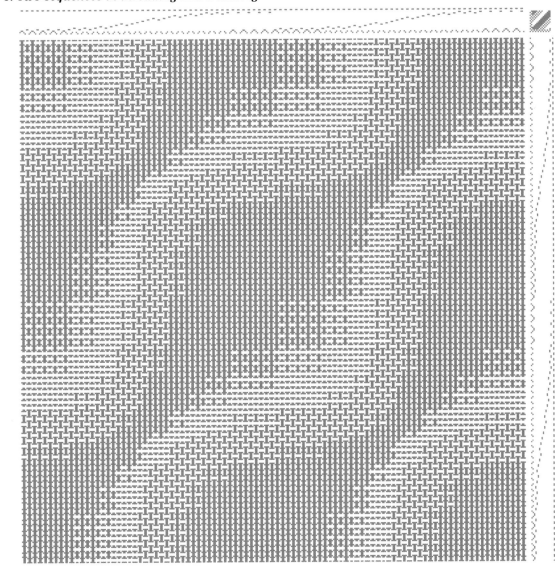

A color-and-weave drawdown of the last example in 4b is repeated once in warp and once in the weft to show the joining of motifs in multiple repeats. Compare with the finished throw, p. 21, and the huck curtains in The Best of Weaver's: Huck Lace, *p. 59.*

Note the large scope of the design and the unusual curved lines that are produced by the networked draft. Shaded areas separate the pattern from the background but do not disrupt the shape of the curves.

Thick and thin threads

A further rule for diversified plain weave is that ends on shafts 1 and 2 must be thin, and ends on the remaining shafts must be thick. Good results can be obtained by using two or three strands as a single working thick warp end as indicated in *3c* and *3d*, p. 20, placing the strands adjacent to each other on the same shaft but each in its own heddle. Various denting schemes can be used, see *3a–d*.

Color arrangements

Maximum patterning effect is obtained when the thick warp and thin weft are of one tonal value and the thick weft and thin warp are of a second, strongly contrasting tonal value. For example, a white thick warp and black thin warp combined with a cream thin weft and navy thick weft work well. On the face of the cloth dark pattern appears on light ground, and on the reverse side the opposite: light pattern on dark ground (see p. 11 for color effects with thick 'n thin).

In diversified plain weave drafts, designs can be treadled as-drawn-in, or treadling schemes can be borrowed from other diversified plain weave drafts for the appropriate number of shafts. In the treadling, picks 1, 3, 4, and 6 of every 6-pick sequence are thin, and the remaining picks (2 and 5) are thick.

Deriving the tie-up

Tie-ups must be carefully constructed according to the following rules: Treadles 1 and 2 raise all of the shafts in alternate order for the thin picks; see the tie-up in *4a*. Shafts 1 and 2 are tied alternately to the pattern treadles to operate the thin warp threads. The remaining area of the tie-up, which determines whether the thick warp or the thick weft appears on the face of the cloth, can contain marked squares in any desired arrangement. With networked threading drafts, however, best results are obtained if this area of the tie-up contains a twill arrangement; see the variations in *4b*. Various all-dark, all-light, or halftone effects are produced in the cloth depending on which twill tie-ups are chosen. Twill tie-ups with fewer interlacement points (such as a 6/8 twill) produce strongly contrasting dark and light areas in the cloth; twill tie-ups that produce more interlacements (such as a 3/1/1/1/1/3/1/1/1/1 twill) produce a cloth with more halftone areas. All of these variations are structurally sound, since interlacement of warp and weft is guaranteed by the alternate threading and treadling of the thin threads. As with any networked draft, transition areas between pattern and background have a fuzzy appearance. These add a distinctive character to the design; see *5*.

This article is dedicated to the memory of Klara Cherepov—A. S. ✄

6. 8-shaft alternate draft

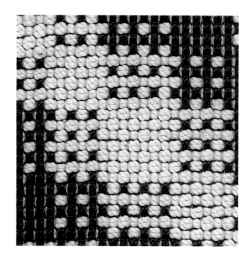

Here is an alternate draft for the blanket that produces a very similar design on eight shafts instead of sixteen. Follow the directions given for the 16-shaft blanket except:

Thread the repeat 12x.

Weave as drawn in for about 60" (substitute treadle numbers for the shaft numbers in the threading draft). For every three picks of weft, use light gray cotton for the first and third picks; use two strands of brick Shetland wound together on the bobbin for the second pick. Follow the finishing directions given for the 16-shaft blanket.

COZY THROWS IN DIVERSIFIED PLAIN WEAVE

Networked diversified plain weave is suitable for many purposes—in the appropriate yarns and setts. Since long floats do not occur on either side, no matter how large the scale of the pattern, the structure makes excellent blankets, upholstery, table linens, and apparel fabrics. The undulating curves of network drafting tend to produce large-scale patterns, so one must be careful here; a design that works well on the king-size bed in your 20' x 30' bedroom might not be appropriate for your baby niece's ski jacket.

This blanket employs the same threading draft as the networked huck lace curtains in *The Best of Weaver's: Huck Lace*, p. 61, except that in the blanket, threads on shafts 1 and 2 are thin and threads on the remaining shafts are a doubled thick yarn. Each strand of the thick yarn is threaded in its own heddle, so *two* heddles are required for each thick working warp end. Thick yarns are doubled on the bobbin for the thick weft. The sett is also different from the lace sett. The blanket is treadled as-drawn-in; epi = ppi. The amounts and directions given here produce two 38" x 54" afghans or nap blankets.

- ❑ Equipment. 16-shaft loom, at least 44" weaving width; 12-dent reed; 2 shuttles; sewing machine.
- ❑ Materials. Warp: 2-ply wool (2000 yds/lb, Shetland, Harrisville), oatmeal, 2 lb; 20/2 pearl cotton, (8400 yds/lb, Halcyon), charcoal, ½ lb. Weft: 2-ply Shetland wool, rust, 2 lb; 20/2 pearl cotton, light gray, ½ lb. This is enough for 2 blankets plus 1 yd loom waste and some sampling. If you want the two blankets to be different colors, purchase 1 lb each of two different dark-value Shetland colors (same light gray cotton used for both). For the binding, purchase 1 yd of silk or polyester taffeta in desired color for each blanket; sewing thread.
- ❑ Wind a warp 6 yds long of 528 ends Shetland and 528 ends 20/2 cotton by holding a strand of each in your hand, keeping them separate with a finger and treating them as one in the threading cross. Put the threading cross at one end and a raddle cross at the other. Spread warp in raddle at a density of 24 epi (12 thick/12 thin), at a width of 44".
- ❑ Beam the warp.
- ❑ Thread the heddles according to the draft in *7*, picking the thick or thin end from the cross as needed. Thread c–d 1x, a–d 5x, and a–b 1x.
- ❑ Sley 2/dent (1 thick and 1 thin) in a 12-dent reed, 24 epi (12 thin, 6 doubled thick). Center for 44".
- ❑ Fasten warp to cloth beam.
- ❑ Weave the cloth at 24 ppi (12 thin/6 doubled thick), using tie-up in *7* and treadling as-drawn-in (substitute treadle numbers for shaft numbers in the threading draft). For every three picks of weft, use light gray cotton for the first and third picks; use two strands of brick Shetland wound together on bobbin for the second pick. Weave from c–d 1x, a–d 6x, and a–b 1x. It is difficult to produce neat selvedges in this combination of weave and materials, and warp fringes are unsatisfactory. Don't worry, all four edges will be covered by binding.
- ❑ Finish by cutting fabric from loom; secure ends by serging or zigzagging on sewing machine. Wash fabric gently by hand in warm water with mild detergent or machine wash delicate cycle with *only 10 sloshes of the agitator—use no further agitation.* Spin out excess water. Rinse and spin out excess water again. Hang blanket to dry. Estimate 14% take-up and shrinkage. Steam press.
- ❑ Cut binding material in 3"-wide strips on straight grain of fabric, piecing where necessary. Machine-stitch binding to blanket with ¾" seam allowance, fold around edge, fold under ¾" on remaining edge of binding, and neatly hand sew in place on reverse side. Either side can be the right side.
- ❑ Cover yourself with this little blanket and take a nap. Then make the second blanket. ✄

thick &thin thick & thin thick & thin thick & thin thick & thin thick & thin thick & thin thick & thin thick & thin thick & thin thick & thin thick & thin thick & thin thick & thin
thick & thin thick & thin thick & thin thick & thin thick & thin thick & thin thick & thin thick & thin thick & thin thick & thin
thin thick & thin thick & thin thick & thin thick & thin thick & thin thick & thin thick & thin thick & thin thick & thin thick & thin thick & thin thick & thin thick & th
thick &thin thick & thin thick & thin thick & thin thick & thin thick & thin thick & thin thick & thin thick & thin thick & thin thick & thin thick & thin thick & thin

7. Networked draft for cozy throw

Thread:
c to d 1x
a to d 5x
a to b 1x.

Sley 1 thick
and 1 thin thread
in each dent of a
12-dent reed.

**Treadle as-
drawn-in:**
c to d 1x
a to d 6x
a to b 1x.

Use light gray cotton
for the thin weft; use
doubled strands of
Harrisville Shetland
for the thick weft.

**Use this draft for a throw in diversified plain weave or experiment with other materials and other
setts for more delicate fabrics. To turn the same draft into huck lace for a future project, tie a new
warp to the old one (drop one of every pair of thick ends), wind on, re-sley to the appropriate epi
for lace (usually a plain weave sett or slightly looser; see The Best of Weaver's Huck Lace, pp. 58±61.**

Christmas table runners

Tracy Kaestner Tracy Kaestner Tracy Kaestner Tracy Kaestner Tracy Kaestner Tracy Kaestner **Tracy Kaestner** Tracy Kaestn

1. Draft for runners

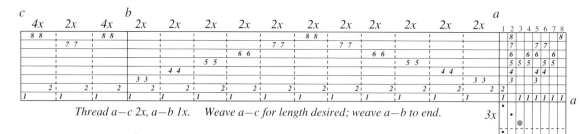

Thread a—c 2x, a—b 1x.   Weave a—c for length desired; weave a—b to end.

Colors of burgundy and forest green with a hint of metallic set the mood for not-so-far-off winter evenings in front of the fire. Get a start on the next holiday season and weave a run of runners. Amounts here are for four small runners, 14" x 26–32". For larger runners, add repeats in both threading and treadling directions.

2. Profile draft for runners

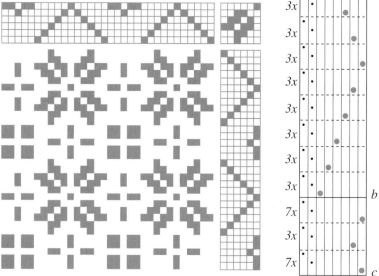

❑ Preparation time. One week and one weekend.

❑ Equipment. 8-shaft loom, 15" weaving width; 12-dent reed; 2 shuttles.

❑ Materials. Thick warp: 3/2 pearl cotton (1260 yds/lb), burgundy ¾ lb, forest green ¼ lb. Thin warp: 20/2 pearl cotton (8400 yds/lb), natural 3 oz. Thick weft: 3/2 pearl cotton in contrasting colors (white, black, and green for these runners), 8 oz. Thin weft: gold metallic supported singles (500 yds/tube, Robin and Russ), 2 tubes. Thin weft for hems: 20/2 pearl cotton in colors coordinating with thick weft, about 25 yds per runner.

Saturday AM:

Wind a warp of 172 ends 3/2 cotton 5 yds long in color order: 44 burgundy, 20 green, 44 burgundy, 20 green, and 44 burgundy. Add 2 burgundy ends, one each side, for floating selvedges, weighted separately. Wind a second warp of 172 ends natural 20/2 cotton. Sley 1 thick end in each dent of a 12-dent reed; center for 14¾". Place a stick or cord over the thick warp and fasten the stick to the reed (on the side that will be next to the breast beam) to keep the two warps separate, and sley 1 thin end in each dent above the stick (1 thick/1 thin in each dent).

Saturday PM:

Thread following the draft in *1*. Thread the thin ends on shafts 1 and 2 and the thick ends on shafts 3–8. Note that two adjacent thick ends are threaded in separate heddles on the same shaft. Be especially careful to keep the threads in order; i.e., make sure that thick and thin ends from the same dent are threaded on adjacent heddles. Beam both warps on a single beam; maintain firm tension during beaming, but take care not to break the 20/2 ends.

Sunday:

Begin weaving the runners using a coordinating 20/2 thread for a 1" turn-under hem using treadles 1 and 2. Alternate a thick weft (white, black, or green) with the metallic weft for the body of each runner. Follow the treadling sequence for desired length; begin and end with the star motif; finish with 1" hem.

For different effects, experiment with different colors of thick wefts, thin wefts, or both. Try treadling 'as-drawn-in' (use the treadle number that corresponds to each shaft number in the threading draft). Begin with treadle 2, for example, then 3, then 3, then 1 (repeat), and continue. Note that a thin weft is used with treadles 1 and 2, a thick weft with 3–8. In order to insert two thick picks in the same shed (to correspond with doubled ends in the threading), pass the shuttle through the shed, around the floating selvedge, and back through the same shed.

Monday – Friday

Finish weaving the runners. To avoid breaking the fine warp threads, weave with relatively loose tension; squeeze the weft in with the beater, change sheds, and squeeze again, rather than beating forcefully.

Saturday

Cut runners off the loom. Serge or machine zigzag between runners and cut apart. Machine wash warm on delicate cycle; hang to dry.

Sunday:

Turn under hems and blindstitch. Now you're ready for Christmas—well, almost! ✄

Now's the time to think of Christmas! Weave these little runners to decorate your holiday table or to give as gifts. Change the colors and/or choose a different 6-block profile draft for other holiday motifs.

hearts and flowers scarves

Marina O'Connor Marina O'Connor Marina O'Connor Marina O'Connor **Marina O'Connor** Marina O

1. Draft for scarves

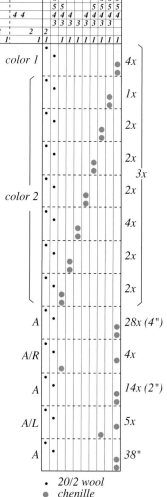

The luxury of rayon chenille and rich jewel-tone colors combine to make these scarves both a weaver's and a wearer's delight. This version of diversified plain weave provides six blocks on eight shafts; many different designs can be woven on the same threading. Both of these scarves use the same tie-up; the only difference is in the treadling order of the blocks. Other designs can be created by changes in both the tie-up and treadling. With more than one working strand in the weft, different colors can be placed in different blocks, side by side.

This dense, warm fabric combining the warmth of wool and the silky luxury of rayon chenille is ideal for scarves. The structure is the 'new' diversified plain weave (see pp. 8–11). Rayon chenille doubled but threaded in separate adjoining heddles is used for each working thick warp thread; two picks of rayon chenille in the same shed compose the thick weft. A fine 2-ply wool (20/2) is used for the thin thread in both warp and weft. Because the chenille yarn appears thicker than it actually is (the yarn itself is the thin inner core, surrounded by rayon fluff), the sett needs to be quite close.

The designs in both scarves use the same threading and tie-up. By varying only the treadling and the weft colors, many designs are possible.

To double the chenille weft, pass the shuttle through the shed, around the floating selvedge, and back through the same shed. Note that since two actual weft passes make one pick of the thick yarn, it is possible to treadle so that the weft color of one of the passes appears on the face in selected blocks and a different color on the face in other blocks (see the motifs between vertical bands of color in the scarves). To do this, throw the shuttle with the first color in the first pattern shed. Then make a second pattern shed and throw a second shuttle with a second color.

HEARTS AND FLOWERS SCARVES

❏ Equipment. 8-shaft loom, 10" weaving width; 8-dent reed; 2 boat shuttles with several bobbins.
❏ Materials. Thick warp for both scarves: rayon chenille (1450 yds/lb, Webs), black ¾ lb. Thin warp and weft–for both scarves: 20/2 wool (5600 yds/lb, Maine Line, JaggerSpun), black 6 oz. Thick weft for Hearts scarf: rayon chenille, Amethyst 5 oz, small amounts of Red, Red Purple, and Light Lilac (Light Lilac is from Fiber Studio, Henniker, NH). Thick weft for Flowers scarf: rayon chenille, Iris 5 oz, small amounts Royal, Azure, Aquamarine, Dark Teal, and Spice.

❏ Wind a warp of 182 black chenille ends and 182 wool ends 5½ yds long. Add 1 wool end to each side for floating selvedges, 366 total ends.
❏ Sley 2 chenille and 2 wool ends/dent in an 8-dent reed, 32 epi; center for 10". Sley floating selvedges in a separate dent on each side.
❏ Thread following the draft in *1:* thread fine wool ends on shafts 1 and 2; thread rayon chenille ends on shafts 3–8. (Adjacent rayon chenille ends on the same shaft are threaded through separate heddles.)
❏ Weave following the treadling in *1* and then in *2* (see p. 30) for about 72" for each scarf. (Note that the contrasting color from the other side will show through a bit while you're weaving, but it disappears when the fabric is dampened and fluffed in the dryer.) Allow 10" for fringe at the beginning and end of each scarf. For Hearts scarf, patterned borders are 17" at each end; weave center portion about 38" long. For Flowers scarf, patterned borders are about 21" at each end; weave center portion about 30" long. (Because of the close sett and the fuzziness of the chenille, it may be necessary to weight the first shaft to keep it from floating up during weaving.)
❏ Finish by removing scarves from the loom and cutting apart. For twisted fringe, twist two groups of 4 ends (2 chenille and 2 wool each) very hard in one direction. (A fringe twister is helpful as it provides maximum twist.) Tie together with an overhand knot about ½" from the ends and allow to twist together in the opposite direction, smoothing and guiding the twist with your fingers. (Chenille fringe requires an extra-tight twist; if it isn't twisted tightly enough, it can loop and deform as it spins in the dryer.) Immerse scarves in lukewarm water just long enough to wet them. Squeeze out (do not wring) excess water; spin out remainder in machine. Tumble dry at medium setting. Finished dimensions are 9¾" x 62". ✂

A = Amethyst,
R = Red,
L = Light Lilac,
P = Red Purple

For colors 1 and 2:
for 1st repeat: 1 = R, 2 = R
2nd repeat 1 = L/R, 2 = L
3rd repeat 1 = P/L, 2 = P

After 38" section, reverse block order for border at other side.

thin thick 'n thin thick 'n thin thick 'n thin thick 'n thin thick 'n thin thick 'n thin thick 'n thin thick 'n thin thick 'n thin thick 'n thin thick 'r
thin thick 'n thin thick 'n thin thick 'n thin thick 'n thin thick 'n thin thick 'n thin thick 'n thin thick 'n thin thick 'n thin thick 'n thin thick 'n
thick 'n thin thick 'n thin thick 'n thin thick 'n thin thick 'n thin thick 'n thin thick 'n thin thick 'n thin thick 'n thin thick 'n thin thick 'n thin thick
thick 'n thin thick 'n thin thick 'n thin thick 'n thin thick 'n thin thick 'n thin thick 'n thin thick 'n thin thick 'n thin thick 'n thin thick 'n thin th

r Marina O'Connor Marina O'Connor Marina O'Connor Marina O'Connor Marina O'Connor Marina

k 'n thin thick 'n thin thick 'n thin thick 'n thin thick 'n thin thick 'n thin thick 'n thin thick 'n thin thick 'n thin thick 'n thin thick 'n thin thick
ck 'n thin thick 'n thin thick 'n thin thick 'n thin thick 'n thin thick 'n thin thick 'n thin thick 'n thin thick 'n thin thick 'n thin thick 'n thin
thin thick 'n thin thick 'n thin thick 'n thin thick 'n thin thick 'n thin thick & thin thick 'n thin thick 'n thin thick 'n thin thick 'n thin thick 'n thin
k 'n thin thick 'n thin thick 'n thin thick 'n thin thick 'n thin thick 'n thin thick 'n thin thick 'n thin thick 'n thin thick 'n thin thick 'n thin
k 'n thin thick 'n thin thick 'n thin thick 'n thin thick 'n thin thick 'n thin thick 'n thin thick 'n thin thick 'n thin thick 'n thin

for Flowers

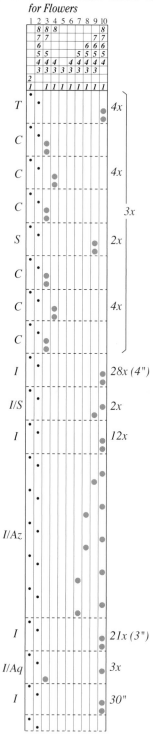

Aq = Aquamarine,
Az = Azure, R = Royal,
S = Spice, T = Dark Teal, I = Iris

For 1st repeat, C = Royal
2nd repeat, C = Azure
3rd repeat, C = Aquamarine

Weave following treadling; after
30" section, reverse block order
for border at other side.

30

log cabin with thick 'n thin

Mauricette Stwalley *Mauricette Stwalley* *Mauricette Stwalley* **Mauricette Stwalley** *Mauricette Stwalley*

BLOUSE AND SLEEVELESS TOP

1. Log cabin draft

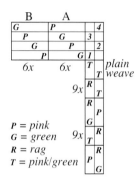

These garments were inspired by an article in the winter 1986 issue of Shuttle, Spindle & Dyepot describing the 'California Rag' technique created by Trudie Roberts. A simple plain weave structure is used to produce a drapable fabric (perfect for tops or vests) that shows the printed designs in the rag weft fabric. Threaded in log cabin, warp colors add to the overall effect.

2. Neck opening

3. Blouse with sleeves

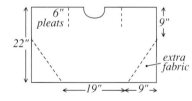

4. Sleeveless top

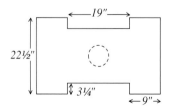

❑ Equipment. 4-shaft loom, 42" weaving width; 8-dent reed; 1 boat shuttle; 1 ski shuttle; rotary cutter with cutting mat; straight edge; pins; #5 16" and 29" circular knitting needles; #8 crochet hook; tapestry needle.

❑ Materials. Warp and thin weft: 8/2 cotton (3360 yds/lb), pink, 12 oz; 10/2 cotton (4200 yds/lb), green, 7¼ oz. Rag weft: 4 yds 100% cotton fabric, bold print. For ribbing: 8/2 cotton, pink, 3 oz; 10/2 cotton, green and dark pink, 2-3 oz ea. Stabilizer such as Pellon Stitch-n-Tear, ½ yd; elastic thread.

❑ Wind a warp of 334 ends 3 yds long with one end 8/2 pink and one end 10/2 green held together.

❑ Sley 1/dent in 8-dent reed; center for 41¾".

❑ Thread following the draft in *1*.

❑ Weave following the draft in *1*. To prepare rags, press fabric (I do not prewash). Fabric strips remain attached at one selvedge to keep in order. Fold the fabric lengthwise with the top selvedge ½" from the lower selvedge. Fold the fabric a second time, again ½" from the lower selvedge. Pin with straight pins along the fold every foot. On cutting mat, with straight edge and rotary cutter, make one cut perpendicular to selvedges to get an even starting edge. Put a safety pin at the corner of the lower selvedge to mark the first strip (this will be the first strip used as weft). Cut the strip 1 cm wide, *do not cut through lower ½" selvedge*. Move straight edge, cut second strip, etc. Remove straight pins as necessary. When you have cut as many strips as you want to start weaving with, cut through the lower selvedge, separating the section of strips. Again, put a safety pin at the corner of the lower selvedge of the uncut cloth to mark where to start cutting for the next section of strips.

a) Remove pin from first strip and with ski shuttle insert strip in shed R. With fingers turn fabric right-side up. Starting at joined fabric selvedge, fold fabric strip right side out and scallop across the shed. Bring the beater up to the strip. Change shed, and beat. *b)* With boat shuttle insert 8/2 weft yarn, change shed and beat firmly. Repeat *a* and *b*. One selvedge shows loose ends of strips, the other the uncut fabric selvedge. Keep this side even so that the pattern lines up correctly. Continue for 84".

❑ Finish by machine zigzagging all four edges. Machine wash, gentle cycle, warm, with mild detergent; machine dry on permanent press. Steam press fabric on cotton setting. Trim selvedges outside of zigzagging.

❑ Cut and assemble by first making patterns in muslin following *2–4* to check fit and shape. For blouse with sleeves (fabric piece 44" x 37"), trace the desired neck shape on stabilizer as in 2, position, and pin on wrong side of fabric. Machine zigzag around neck shape, cut out, roll, and hem. Make shoulder pleats ⅝" wide and 12" long; baste; machine straight stitch. Fold garment wrong side out. Pin side seams. With straight edge and dress-marking pencil, draw a diagonal line from sleeve pin to waist pin. Pin on this line. Baste slightly off line to remove basting thread easily. Machine straight stitch; measure ¾" from side seam and mark with dress-marking pencil and straight edge on four areas to cut extra side seam fabric away. Machine zigzag with a stabilizer; cut extra fabric off. Roll and hem; press side seams.

With single strand of 10/2 green cotton, crochet a chain at the waist, neck, and arms. *a)* At the waist, with 29" circular knitting needle pick up 180 stitches. (For knitting use two strands 8/2 pink cotton as one, 1 strand 10/2 green, and 1 strand 10/2 dark pink.) Knit rib of k2, p2, for 2½". Bind off. With tapestry needle, sew elastic thread loosely at top and bottom of ribbing on wrong side. *b)* At the neck, with 16" needle pick up 128 stitches. Knit rib ½", purl one row all around, knit rib 1". Bind off. Turn at purl row to the inside and hemstitch with needle and thread. *c)* At the sleeve, with 16" needle pick up 80 stitches. Knit rib 3". Bind off. Roll up cuff and stitch. Repeat for other sleeve.

For sleeveless top cut and assemble with stabilizer as in *4*. Prepare knit and crochet finish as for blouse except *a)* at the waist pick up 196 stitches. *b)* At the neck knit rib for 6" to form turtleneck. *c)* At one arm, with 16" needle, pick up 75 stitches. (Pick up around arm, but not under.) On first row of ribbing, start with p2, then increase in next stitch with k2 to end up with 100 stitches. Knit rib for 2". Bind off. Sew ribbing to under arm. Repeat for other arm. ✄

thick 'n thin thick 'n thin

cette Stwalley Mauricette Stwalley Mauricette Stwalley Mauricette Stwalley Mauricette Stwalley Maur

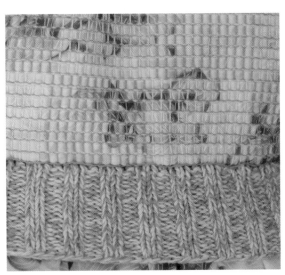

beyond log cabin

Erica de Ruiter Erica de Ruiter Erica de Ruiter Erica de Ruiter Erica de Ruiter **Erica de Ruiter** Erica de

COLOR-AND-WEAVE WITH THICK AND THIN

Color-and-weave effects in plain weave or basket weave are achieved by alternating dark and light fibers of the same size in both warp and weft, as in familiar log cabin or in the design we call 'hound's tooth.' Add thin threads to both warp and weft and gain even more dramatic and versatile patterning—on as few as two shafts!

When thick and thin threads alternate, thick dark or light warp threads can be raised for successive thick picks since they interlace with the thin weft throughout. Thick dark or light weft threads can pass over or under successive thick warp threads since they interlace with the thin warp throughout.

In addition, the alternation of thick and thin threads produces a very supple fabric. The colors of the thin yarns can subtly influence the thick yarns; shiny or metallic thin threads can add a festive effect. The thick black and white matte wool yarns in samples *a–d* gain luster from a thin lurex yarn. In *e–f*, very dark thin threads frame the light and dark thick threads.

Tips for thick and thin

The thin yarn should either be neutral or related in in hue to the colors of the thick threads that produce the color-and-weave effect. Medium dark or dark thin threads usually produce the best results. Bleached white can be used successfully for the thin threads when the thick yarns consist of bleached white and a pastel, as in the project towels; see p. 35. Otherwise, instead of white, choose off-white, natural, or unbleached thin yarns.

The thick and thin yarns can be beamed together on the same warp beam. Keep the warp under tension when beaming to prevent twisting and tangling. Sett the thick yarn as for a relatively loose plain weave; sley each thin yarn in the same dent of the reed as the adjacent thick yarn. Always check setts and fabric hand by sampling.

When using doubled threads for the thick yarns, which gives very good results, thread each of the two strands in separate heddles (on the same shaft) and where possible sley each in a separate dent. To double a weft, weave each single strand separately, passing the shuttle around the floating selvedge and back into the same shed. The thick threads are doubled strands of yarn in the drafts in *2–4* (p. 36) and in the project towels.

a. Hound's tooth design

b. Large lover's knot design

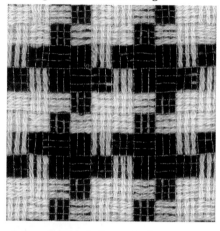

c. Small hound's tooth design

d. Small lover's knot design

e. Lattice design

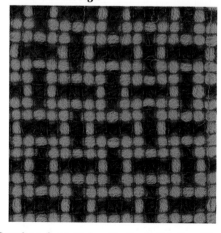

f. Variation of lattice design

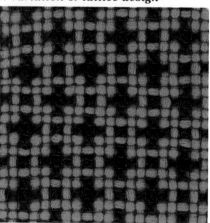

*Samples **a–b** are produced by the draft in **2**, p. 36; samples **c–d** by the draft in **3**; and samples **e–j** by the draft in **4**. The thick threads in all of the samples are a doubled 7/2 wool (1700 yds/lb): black and white in **a–d**; red and dark purple (aubergine) in **e–f**; dark blue and light blue in **g–j**. The thin threads are a multicolored lurex in **a–d**, a dark purple 30/2 cotton in **e–f**, and a gray-brown acrylic in **g–j**.*

'n thin thick 'n thin

Erica de Ruiter Erica de Ruiter Erica de Ruiter Erica de Ruiter Erica de Ruiter Erica de Ruiter Erica de Ruiter Erica de

Erica's clever threading produces a surprisingly complex design– on only two shafts. Weave these towels in traditional blue and white for a country kitchen or use a mix of bright colors for a contemporary look.

k 'n thin thick 'n thin thick 'n thin thick 'n thin thick 'n thin thick 'n thin thick 'n thin thick 'n thin thick 'n thin thick 'n thin thic
thin thick 'n thin thick 'n thin thick 'n thin thick 'n thin thick 'n thin thick 'n thin thick 'n thin thick 'n thin thick 'n thin thick 'n thin thic
k 'n thin thick 'n thin thick 'n thin thick 'n thin thick 'n thin thick & thin thick 'n thin thick 'n thin thick 'n thin thick 'n thin thick 'n thin thick 'n
k 'n thin thick 'n thin thick 'n thin thick 'n thin thick 'n thin thick 'n thin thick 'n thin thick 'n thin thick 'n thin thick 'n thin thick 'n thin thic

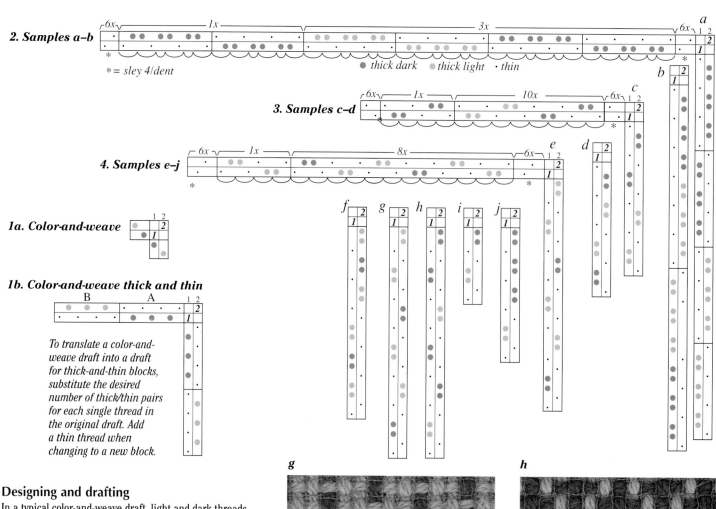

2. Samples a–b

* = sley 4/dent

● *thick dark* ● *thick light* · *thin*

3. Samples c–d

4. Samples e–j

1a. Color-and-weave

1b. Color-and-weave thick and thin

To translate a color-and-weave draft into a draft for thick-and-thin blocks, substitute the desired number of thick/thin pairs for each single thread in the original draft. Add a thin thread when changing to a new block.

Designing and drafting

In a typical color-and-weave draft, light and dark threads of the same size fiber alternate in the threading and treadling. The alternation can be every other thread (D-L-D-L, as in the abbreviated draft in *1a*) or a multitude of other arrangements (D-D-L-L, D-D-L-D-D-L, etc.). This crossing of warp and weft colors produces a visual pattern that does not appear to be related to the structural interlacement.

Any color-and-weave draft that can be produced on a plain weave threading can be enlarged to become a 2-block design in thick and thin. To translate a standard color-and-weave draft into a draft for color-and-weave with thick and thin threads: Substitute as many thick/thin warp pairs as desired for each dark or light thread in the original color-and-weave threading draft and as many thick/thin weft pairs as desired for each dark or light weft in the original color-and-weave treadling draft. For example, each thread in *1a* becomes three thick threads in *1b*. Begin and end each threading block with a thin thread on the opposite shaft from the shaft of the thin thread in the adjacent block. Begin and end each treadling block with a thin pick using the opposite treadle from the treadle in the adjacent block. Note that in *2–5*, the thick threads are doubled strands of yarn.

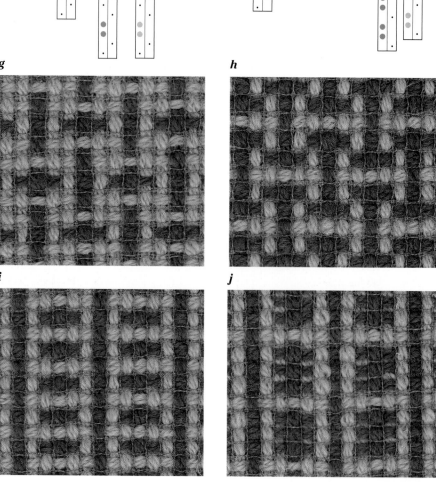

5a. Draft for towels

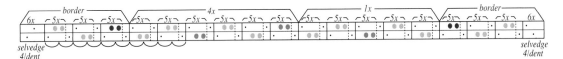

5c. Denting order of 5x repeats in 5a

Sley one thick end in every dent; sley thin ends: 1-0-1-0-1-0-1-1.

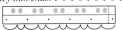

5b. Color order for towels

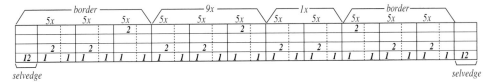

- ● med blue
- ● lt blue
- ● bleached
- · 30/2

5d. Treadling for towels

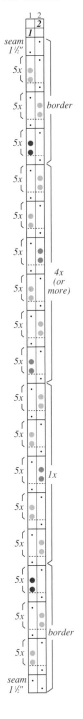

TOWELS IN THICK 'N THIN

Use only two shafts to experiment with 2-block color-and-weave patterns. Try a sampler to test design ideas and then weave a set of decorative towels. The alternate use of thick and thin threads provides unexpected softness and absorbency for towels, and a drapable fabric for other uses.

The samples

- ❑ Equipment. 2-shaft loom, 12" weaving width for all three samplers; 10-dent reed; 3 shuttles.
- ❑ Materials. Thick warp and weft: 7/2 wool (1700 yds/lb, Klippans, Glimåkra Looms 'n Yarns), one dark color, one light color, 2 oz each color for 2 yd warp. Colors used for these samples are: black and off-white (*a–d*); red and dark purple (*e–f*); light blue and dark blue (*g–j*). Thin warp and weft: sewing thread or fine cotton (30/2 or finer), firmly spun fine wool (30/2 or finer), or strong metallic thread, 400 yds for 2-yd warp.
- ❑ Wind warps of 48 thick dark ends, 36 thick light ends, 80 thin ends for *a–b*; 44 thick dark ends, 40 thick light ends, 108 thin ends for *c–d*; 32 dark, 68 light, 124 thin for *e–j*, 2 yds long each.
- ❑ Sley each warp as indicated by the drafts in *2–4*; center *a–b* and *c–d* for 9", *e–j* for 10⅔".
- ❑ Thread following the drafts in *2–4*.
- ❑ Beam on a single beam, maintaining firm tension during beaming.
- ❑ Weave following the treadling sequences *a–j* in *2–4*. Experiment with other treadling orders.

6. Hanging tag for towels

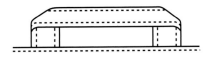

The towels

- ❑ Equipment. 2-shaft loom, 25" weaving width; 15-dent reed; 3 shuttles.
- ❑ Materials. Amounts given are for four towels. Thick warp and weft: 5/2 pearl cotton (2100 yds/lb), white 1 lb; medium blue 2 oz; light blue ½ lb. Thin warp and weft: 30/2 bleached cotton (12,600 yds/lb), 4 oz, or white sewing thread, approximately 2000 yds.
- ❑ Wind a warp of 240 ends 5/2 white, 20 ends 5/2 blue, 90 ends 5/2 light blue. Wind a warp of 234 ends 30/2 cotton or sewing thread.
- ❑ Sley one 5/2 end in each dent of a 15-dent reed following the color order in *5b*; center for 23⅓". Sley the 30/2 cotton (or sewing thread) in the following order: 12 selvedge ends at 4/dent using the 3 empty dents adjacent to the first dents containing the pearl cotton; then (in the dents where the pearl cotton is already sleyed) sley 1-0-1-0-1-0-1-1 in every 10 dents for 35 sections of 10 dents each as in *5c* (check these carefully). End by sleying 12 selvedge ends 4/dent in the 3 dents beyond the pearl cotton at the other edge. Add one 30/2 end each side for floating selvedges.
- ❑ Beam with firm tension.
- ❑ Thread following the draft in *5a*.
- ❑ Weave four towels following treadling sequence in *5d*. Separate each towel with scrap yarn.
- ❑ Finish by removing from loom; cut towels apart. Remove scrap yarn; hand hem. Attach tag as shown in *6* if desired. Machine wash using mild detergent, gentle cycle; lay flat to dry. ✂

thinner, thin, thicker, thickest: color-

Erica de Ruiter Erica de Ruiter Erica de Ruiter Erica de Ruiter Erica de Ruiter Erica de Ruiter **Erica de Ruiter** Erica de R

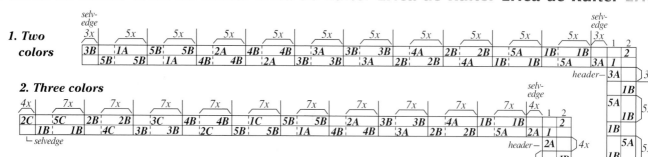

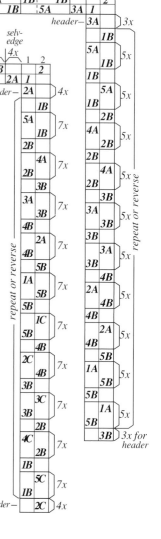

The structure is simple plain weave. The squares of pattern are produced by the color-and-weave effect long known and loved by weavers as log cabin—combined with an alternation of thick and thin yarns. When using several strands of a thin yarn to comprise a thick one, it is possible to change the relative thicknesses of the two alternating warp yarns from one selvedge to the other. In the scarves on p. 39, at one selvedge five thin threads in one color comprise a thick end; the thin end is one thread of a second color. The relative thicknesses of the two working ends change gradually across the warp to become the opposite at the other edge (one end of the first color, five of the second). Use two, three, or even more colors to achieve subtle color variations—all on only two or three shafts!

LOG CABIN THICK TO THIN

If two colors are used and the two alternating ends begin as five strands of Color A and one strand of Color B, then A can be decreased by one thread and B increased by one in each successive section (or 'block'), causing a subtle color change across the fabric in the warp. By treating the weft in the same way, color changes can also occur vertically in the fabric. Astonishing effects are possible on only two shafts with this unusual adaptation of log cabin and thick 'n thin.

Examine the threading draft in *1*. The numbers in the draft indicate the number of thin ends that are warped together, sleyed together, and threaded together through a single heddle to act as one working end. (Three working ends of three strands each in Color A are threaded at each selvedge.) The first log cabin block is threaded: one strand Color B on shaft 2, five strands of Color A on shaft 1 (5x), to end with one strand Color B on shaft 2. In the next section, the same thicknesses of Color B and Color A are threaded but on the opposite shafts, causing the stripes characteristic of log cabin to run in the opposite direction from the first section.

In the third section, two strands of Color B are threaded on shaft 2, four strands of Color A on shaft 1 (5x), to end with two strands of Color B on shaft 2; the fourth section repeats the same thicknesses but on the opposite shafts. The process continues with 3/3, 4/2, and 5/1 as the relative numbers of colors A and B. (A = orange; B = blue in the scarf on the left, p. 39).

The effects are most successful when the two colors contrast strongly in value and hue.

Two-color fabric

Use the following directions to weave a sampler for practice or a drapable scarf.

❑ Equipment. 2-shaft loom, 10" weaving width; 8-dent reed; 10 shuttles (ten different relative numbers of the two colors act as ten different wefts).

❑ Materials. 20/2 pearl cotton (8400 yds/lb) in two colors, 2 oz each color, orange (A) and blue (B) for the scarf fabric at the left on p. 39.

❑ Wind a warp 2½ yds long or as desired for 2-yd sampler or scarf following the color order in *1*. Wind ends singly, but wind the number indicated so that they are together in the cross. For the selvedge, wind three orange (A) strands together in the cross, three times. Then for the first log cabin block, wind 1B by itself in the cross, 5A together, five times, etc., and continue.

❑ Sley 2 working ends/dent in an 8-dent reed: two 3-strand A in the first dent, one 3-strand A and 1B in the second dent, one 5-strand A and 1B in the third dent, etc.

❑ Thread following the draft in *1*. Thread each working end of 1, 2, 3, 4, or 5 strands as indicated together in the heddle.

❑ Wind 5 stick shuttles (boat shuttles with bobbins can also be used) with 1, 2, 3, 4, and 5 strands A, and 5 shuttles with 1, 2, 3, 4, and 5 strands B.

❑ Weave following the draft in *1*, alternating the two shuttles with the indicated number of threads.

❑ Finish by hemstitching or fringing ends; wash by hand in warm water; lay flat to dry; press. For wider fabrics repeat or reverse the pattern.

Three-color fabric

The warp for the 3-color fabric (see the scarf at the right on p. 39) is 30/2 cotton sleyed 2 working ends/dent in a 10-dent reed; the directions are otherwise the same as for the 2-color fabric. Note that the color progresses from Color A with a small amount of Color B, to Color B with a small amount of Color A and then with a small amount of Color C, to Color C with a small amount of Color B. Color B is used throughout the fabric; try mixing Colors A and C for even more variation.

Use different colors from those shown here, use heavier fibers for table mats, wools for blankets and clothing, and experiment with more colors! ✄

and-weave on two shafts

Three colors change thicknesses in both warp and weft for this fabric. One warp color, yellow, is dominant at the right edge; red-violet becomes dominant at the center; purple becomes dominant at the left edge. When the same gradation occurs in the weft, the color changes appear subtle and complex.

Only two shafts (and no complicated dye techniques) are required for this fabric! The subtle color effects are created by gradually changing the relative thicknesses of warp and weft yarns in the warping and weaving process. Use these drapable fabrics for scarves or clothing, or weave them in thicker fibers for throws, table mats, upholstery, or rugs.

three blocks on three shafts

Erica de Ruiter Erica de Ruiter Erica de Ruiter Erica de Ruiter Erica de Ruiter Erica de Ruiter Erica de R

Three blocks on three shafts! It is hard to believe that any pattern weave can give so much for so little! The use of thick and thin warp and weft threads allows the thick warp (dark) or the thick weft (light) to appear on the surface to form pattern or background.

1. Profile draft: *see Photo a, p. 41*

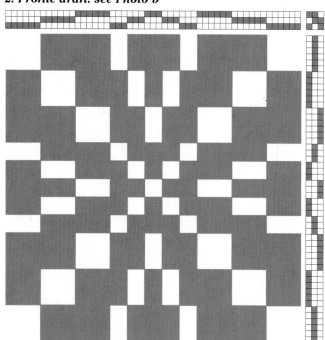

2. Profile draft: *see Photo b*

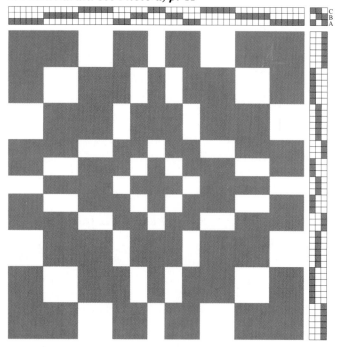

3. Profile draft: *see Photo c*

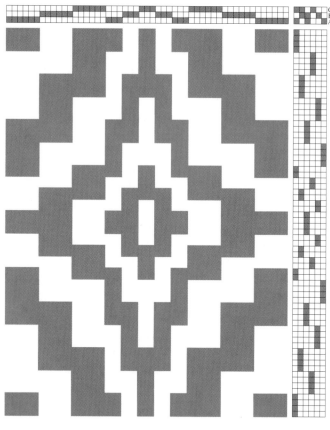

4. Profile draft: *see Photo d*

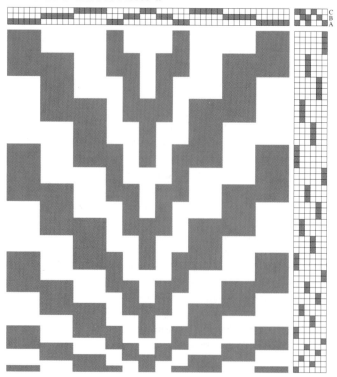

thick 'n thin thick 'n thin thick 'n thin thick 'n thin thick 'n thin thick 'n thin thick 'n thin thick 'n thin thick 'n thin thick 'n thin thick 'n thin thick 'n thin thick 'n thin thick 'n thin thick 'n thin thick 'n thin thick 'n thin thick 'n

Erica de Ruiter Erica de Ruiter Erica de Ruiter Erica de Ruiter Erica de Ruiter Erica de Ruiter Erica de Ruiter Erica de

5. Threading for sampler

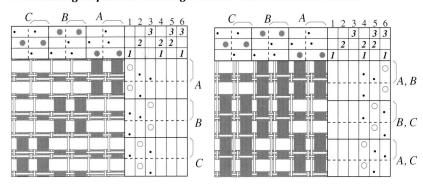

6. Treadling sequences for single blocks and combined blocks

Repeat bracketed sections for block width and length desired.

This structure is related to diversified plain weave (see pp. 8–11), in which thin warp ends are threaded on shafts 1 and 2 and thick warp ends on the remaining shafts (the 'pattern shafts'). The number of potential blocks equals the number of shafts minus two: four shafts provide two blocks, eight shafts provide six.

In this 3-shaft version, all three shafts carry both thick *and* thin ends. Because of the shared shafts, the structure is not a unit weave and cannot be used for threading profile drafts without limitations. Ends must be omitted when changing from one threading block to another, and picks omitted when changing from one treadling block to another.

Examine the threading in *6*. Notice that the threading for A is thick on 1, thin on 2, thin on 3. When changing to Block B, the last end on 3 is omitted to avoid threading two ends in succession on shaft 3. Picks must also be omitted if the block change requires the same shafts to be lifted twice in succession.

Notice that the threading for the sampler in *5* is mirror-image symmetrical—for a perfectly balanced draft, descending blocks are threaded in exactly the reverse order of ascending blocks.

THREE-SHAFT SAMPLER

❑ Equipment. 3-shaft (4-shaft) loom, 8-dent reed; 2 shuttles.
❑ Materials. Thick warp: Victorian 2-ply wool (1475 yds/lb, Halcyon) dark color. Thick weft: Victorian 2-ply wool, light color. Thin warp: light colored sewing thread. Thin weft: dark colored sewing thread. For variety, use metallics for thin weft.
❑ Wind a warp of 51 thick ends and a separate warp of 90 thin ends. (Use lengths as desired for sampling.) Beam the two warps on separate beams, if available, spreading both warps to 6⅛" weaving width (see warping tips for thick and thin threads, pp. 6–7).
❑ Thread following the draft in *5*.
❑ Sley 1 thick end in each dent of an 8-dent reed *with* accompanying sewing thread ends. There will be 2 sewing thread ends in every dent except at block changes (where there will be 1 sewing thread end).
❑ Weave by substituting the treadling sequence in *6* for the block or blocks that corresponds to the block(s) indicated in the selected profile draft. ✄

a. Three shafts, three treadles

c. Three shafts, six treadles

b. Three shafts, three treadles

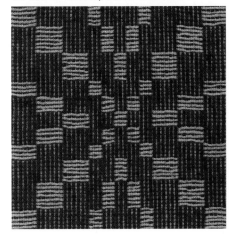

d. Three shafts, six treadles

magic pleats—from eight shafts to two

Erica de Ruiter Erica de Ruiter Erica de Ruiter Erica de Ruiter Erica de Ruiter **Erica de Ruiter** Erica de R

"My favorite challenge is to reduce an interesting draft to fewer than four shafts. On a recent tour through Finland, I discovered a wonderful pleated weave, created by warpway stripes of 3/1 and 1/3 twill. It is a simple matter to reduce the 8-shaft draft to six with stripes of 2/1 and 1/2 twill, but how to achieve a pleated effect on fewer than four?"

The draft for the Finnish fabric requires eight shafts and four treadles as shown in *1*. An experiment to duplicate the pleats with a soft wool warp results in the rainbow striped scarf, p. 43. Even on the loom, the fabric begins to pleat; when immersed in water, the pleats deepen further—like magic!

Pleated fabrics with thick 'n thin

However, Erica would not be Erica if she did not try a 3-shaft version, and even more challenging, a version for two shafts. The natural tendency for the 8-shaft weave to pleat is due to the narrow adjacent stripes of warp-emphasis vs weft-emphasis interlacements: each pulls the fabric in a different direction. I wondered if the same contrast in pull could be produced by a thick 'n thin weave in which stripes of thick warp threads raised continuously for the thick picks alternate with stripes of thick warp threads lowered continuously for the thick picks. A warp goes on the loom, and the answer is 'Yes!'

Twill vs thick 'n thin pleats

There are some surprising differences, however. In the 8-shaft twill version, the warp-emphasis stripes bulge out, weft-emphasis stripes cave in. In the thick 'n thin versions, the weft-emphasis stripes do the bulging. One pleasant advantage to the thick 'n thin versions is that since the thick weft color can be changed at any time, some freedom of design becomes possible during weaving to the stripes that show the most.

It is important that the thick weft threads be very soft to allow the yarns to bulge. The thick 'n thin pleating is slightly less pronounced than with the 8-shaft twill weave, and the fabric is not quite as drapable.

8-SHAFT PLEATED WOOL SCARF

❑ Equipment. 8-shaft loom, 12" weaving width; 10-dent reed; 1 shuttle.
❑ Materials. Warp: 8/2 wool (2240 yds/lb) in assorted rainbow colors, app 2½ oz for the 13 stripes in the scarf on p. 43 (choose a soft wool such as a merino). Weft: 16/2 cotton (6720 yds/lb), black, 1½ oz.

1. 8-shaft draft for pleats

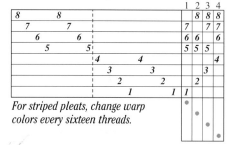

For striped pleats, change warp colors every sixteen threads.

3a. Warping order for 3-shaft thick 'n thin pleats

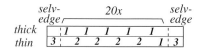

3b. 3-shaft draft for pleats

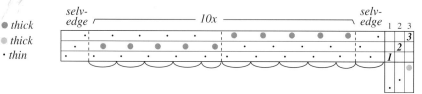

2b. 2-shaft draft for pleats

2a. Warping order for 2-shaft thick 'n thin pleats

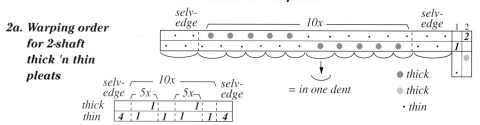

● thick
● thick
· thin

❑ Wind a warp of 16 ends each rainbow color for desired width of scarf, 2½ yds long, 208 total ends for the 13 stripes in this scarf.
❑ Sley 2/dent in a 10-dent reed, 20 epi; center for desired width, 10½" this scarf; add 1 floating selvedge to each side.
❑ Thread following the draft in *1*. Change colors every 16 ends.
❑ Weave following the draft in *1*.
❑ Finish by removing from loom; wash gently in warm water by hand (do not agitate); lay on towels to dry.

PLEATED THICK 'N THIN

Although a thick 'n thin draft on three shafts can be used to produce three pattern blocks (see "Three blocks on Three Shafts," pp. 40-41), pleating happens as a result of two contrasting interlacements rather than three—one warp-emphasis, one weft-emphasis. The only difference between the 2- and 3-shaft drafts is that two thin wefts separate the thick picks in the 3-shaft version, one in the 2-shaft version; compare *2* and *3*.

❑ Equipment. 2-shaft or 4-shaft loom, 10" weaving width; 10-dent reed; 2 shuttles.

❑ Materials. Amounts given here are for a 10" wide warp, 2½ yds long, enough for one scarf. Thick warp: 8/2 cotton (3200 yds/lb), used doubled, 2½ oz total. Thin warp and weft: 20/2 cotton (8400 yds/lb) or 30/2 cotton (12,600 yds/lb), 1½ oz 20/2 (1 oz 30/2) for 3-shaft draft; for 2-shaft draft 1 oz 20/2 (¾ oz 30/2). The thin warp and weft should be a neutral color. Thick weft: 8/2 cotton used doubled, in one or more colors, 2¼ oz total. The thick weft should be very soft in order to form the pleats.
❑ Wind a warp of 100 thick ends doubled 8/2 cotton (200 ends total). Wind a warp of 128 thin ends for the 2-shaft draft in *2b* or 186 thin ends for the 3-shaft draft in *3b*.
❑ Sley one thick end in each dent of a 10-dent reed with accompanying thin ends following the denting diagram in *2b* or *3b*. There will be 2 thin ends in every dent except at each change to a new block, where there will be one thin end (sley the group of three or four selvedge ends in an extra dent on each side).
❑ Thread following the drafts in *2b* or *3b*.
❑ Weave with thick and thin wefts following the treadling sequences in *2b* or *3b*.
❑ Finish as for 8-shaft pleated fabric. ✄

thin thick 'n thin t

Weavers love fabrics that defy the one-dimensional flatness usually characteristic of fabric produced on a loom. We play with textured yarns and weaves that allow long, heavy floats. Imagine the joyful surprise of watching a fabric pleat as you weave– and even more with washing. The colors in the ditches seem to appear and disappear as the cloth flattens and re-pleats.

patchwork rugs

1. 4-shaft, 4-block draft

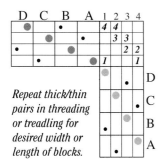

Repeat thick/thin pairs in threading or treadling for desired width or length of blocks.

No warp is too long when you start weaving patchwork rugs because there are so many very attractive possibilities. With a change in the weight or type of warp and weft materials, this weave can also make terrific placemats, tote bags, and even eye-catching fabrics for clothing.

'Patchwork' rugs are decorative, sturdy, flat, and washable. They can be formal or casual, thin or heavy, bold or quiet. There is vitality and harmony in their irregularities. Multicolored in both warp and weft, they are a great way to use up small amounts of yarns. The secret to their deceptive simplicity is the use of thick and thin threads in both warp and weft. The fabrics look marvelously complex, but the structure is easy to thread, weave, and understand. There are unlimited options for color experimentation—even after weaving has begun. Thread once, and weave more than one unique piece on the same warp.

Any 4-shaft loom is suitable for weaving patchwork rugs (the balanced tie-up makes the draft suitable for counterbalance looms; four shafts provide four blocks; see *1*. Pattern is created by selecting either the thick warp threads or the thick weft threads to show on the face of the cloth. Although two blocks always work together, the variety of color options is unlimited and makes the design seem very complex.

Thick 'n thin: four blocks on four shafts

Examine the threading and treadling sequences in *1*. In each block, a thick thread on one shaft is followed by a thin thread on the 'opposite' shaft. (Shafts 1 and 3 are considered opposite to each other since they are in opposite positions on the twill circle; shafts 2 and 4 are opposite to each other.) These thick/thin pairs are repeated as desired to determine the size of each block. The patchwork rugs on p. 45 show blocks of consistent width and height. Varying the width and height of blocks can increase design complexity.

Characteristics of the structure

Note that the thin ends in one block are threaded on the same shaft as the thick ends in the opposite block. (Shaft 1 carries the thick end in Block A and the thin end in Block C, for example.)

Examine the treadling sequence in *1*. Thick and thin weft threads alternate on opposite treadles. In areas where thick weft picks pass over thick warp threads, the thin warp threads bind the wefts tightly for a nearly weft-faced surface. In the areas where thick warp threads pass over thick weft picks, the thin weft picks bind the thick warp threads for a nearly warp-faced surface.

Blocks do not weave pattern or background independently; two are always linked: AB, BC, CD, or DA; see the tie-up in *1*. The first treadle raises thick warp ends in Blocks A and D so that the colors of the thick warp threads appear on the face of the cloth in these blocks and the thick weft thread appears on the face of the cloth in Blocks B and C. On the thin pick with treadle 3 only small flecks of thick warp and thin weft show as subtle color influences. Note that thick warp colors can be different in Blocks A and D, disguising the fact that they operate together.

Follow the rest of the treadling sequence to see how block pairs work together. Note that the color of the thick weft can be changed at any time.

Special features

It is especially effective to use several thin threads together to form the thick thread in the warp. These threads are each drawn through individual heddles on the same shaft to minimize twisting or bunching. Four thin threads act as each working thick warp end in the patchwork project rug; see *2*, p. 46.

When several thin ends are used as a single acting thick end, only one warp beam is required and any warping method can be used. The back-to-front method used for these rugs makes the beaming process especially tangle-free, see p. 45.

Deriving drafts for this thick-and-thin variation is very straightforward. Although patchwork drafts are similar to shadow weave drafts (in which dark and light threads alternate instead of thick and thin threads), they do not require adding or dropping warp or weft threads at turning points.

A patchwork draft cannot form true tabby. For hems and headers, alternate any two opposite treadles (1 vs 3 or 2 vs 4, for example).

The thickness of the fabric depends on warp and weft size, warp tension, and beat. If cloth wefts are used as for the rugs in this project, taper and overlap the wefts in the shed by 3–4". Gluing or sewing the strips together is not necessary. Give the cloth wefts a twist at the selvedge to reduce bulk.

Variations

Experiment with color. Change warp colors with each block change. Mix warp colors within a block—but a bit more cautiously to maintain a coherent design.

Further variations include the threading order of the blocks (one of the most versatile is a symmetrical point, e.g., A, B, C, D, C, B, A); block treadling order (striped, checkered, or jumbled); widths of blocks; heights of blocks (long, short, or mixed blocks); different weft colors every few picks; high contrasts in the prints selected as cloth weft strips; color changes in warp or weft (but observe some limitations; too many changes can result in a design that is too busy).

PHOTO BY AK PHOTO

*Bright warm and soft cool colors make Jane's patchwork rugs an eye-catching addition to any room.
Choose a favorite combination of colors and brighten your winter days±on the loom and on the floor.*

2. Draft for patchwork rugs

This weave leaves you wishing you had put on a longer warp — another experiment is always beckoning. The two patchwork rugs on p. 45 are both woven with the same threading and treadling order of the blocks. In the upper rug, random lengths of colored thick wefts are used and 8 thick picks are made for each block. In the lower rug (the project rug), 10 thick picks of the same cloth weft are made for each block. Any change in color order creates a different design. Darker values are used for the rug below (woven by Jane Evans).

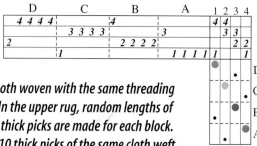

PATCHWORK RUGS

Directions given here produce the lower rug on p. 45. Change warp and/or weft colors for a different-looking rug.

- Equipment. 4-shaft loom, 34" weaving width; 12-dent reed; two stick or ski shuttles (minimum); sewing machine.
- Materials. Warp: 8/4 cotton (1600 yds/lb, Edgemont Yarn Service), 2½ oz each light blue (LB), pink (P), dark blue (DB), dark green (DG); 2¼ oz each lilac (L), sand (S), pale orange (PO); 1½ oz each gold (G), mushroom (M). Weft: for thin weft use 8/4 cotton (1600 yds/lb), sand, 250 yds or 2½ oz; for thick weft use pre-shrunk cloth strips, cotton flannel, ½" wide, 30 yds each light green (LG), light blue (LB), light peach (LP); 20 yds each gold (G), dark orange (DO), dark green (DG). Cotton sewing thread, sand; Fraycheck™ fabric glue.
- Wind a warp of 8/4 cotton 7½ ft long for one rug, arranging the color groups in the following order: 40 LB, 10 P, 40 PO, 10 DG, 40 L, 10 G, 40 DB, 10 LB, 40 S, 10 M, 40 DG, 10 PO, 40 G, 10 S, 40 P, 10 LB, 40 M, 10 DB, 40 L, 10 DG, 40 LB, 10 DB, 40 DG, 10 M, 40 P, 10 L, 40 PO, 10 G, 40 DB, 10 P, 40 S, 10 DG (800 total ends).
- Spread in a raddle and wind onto a single warp beam, centered for 33⅓" width.
- Thread the warp, substituting the threading for each block as shown in the draft in *2* in the following block order (starting with the 40 LB/10 P block): A, B, C, D, A, D, B, C, D, A, B, C, D, C, A, B. In each thick/thin pair four threads of one color make up the thick thread, the single thread in the other color is the thin. Take threads from the color group of 40 for each group of four ends on one shaft, then take an end from the color group of 10 for the single end on one shaft. It will not matter that warp ends cross over each other a bit as they come from the back beam.
- Add 1 end each side (1 LB, 1 DG) for floating selvedges.
- Sley 2/dent in a 12-dent reed for 24 epi.
- Weave following the draft in *2*. Use treadles 1 and 3 alternately for a 2½" hem with the 8/4 cotton weft. Then weave the blocks in the following order: D, C, B, A, D, C, B, A, D, C, B, A, D, C, B (15 blocks). Using the cloth weft for the thick weft and the 8/4 cotton weft for the thin weft, weave 20 total picks for each block using as the color for the thick weft: LG, DO, LB, LP, G, DG, LB, DO, LP, LG, G, LB, DG, LP, LG. Weave the second hem. Advance the warp frequently and avoid extreme tension.
- Finish by gluing ends with Fraycheck. Cut from loom. Machine stitch raw ends carefully. Turn hem ¼", then in half to abut the thick part of rug. Machine stitch next to abutment. Machine soak in hot, soapy water; agitate 1–2 minutes; spin; rinse without agitation; spin. Lay flat to dry, shaping to square. Finished size is 31" x 41". ✄

patchwork is not just for rugs

If you are surprised by the multiblock look of Jane Evans' 4-shaft patchwork rugs (p. 45), you might be even more surprised to discover what a light, soft fabric can be woven from finer threads in both warp and weft. Easy to weave and sew– and very easy to care for– this jacket is always ready to go!

1. Draft for patchwork jacket

B	C	D	C	B	A	1 2 3 4
4		4 4 4 4		4		4 4
	3 3 3 3		3 3 3 3		3	3 3
2 2 2 2		2		2 2 2 2		2 2
	1		1		1 1 1 1 1	1
12x	12x	12x	12x	12x	12x	

← 3x →

A 16x ¥
B 16x ¥
C 16x ¥
D 16x ¥

"This jacket is inspired by the 'Patchwork' rugs, pp. 44–46. Although I am not a rug weaver, I am captivated by the amazing interplay of blocks and colors this structure can provide on only four shafts. I decided to investigate its possible use for garments—and am delighted with the results!"

PATCHWORK JACKET

A 16/2 cotton warp (multiple strands are used for the thick warp threads), a thick weft of soft 8/4 cotton, and a thin weft of 16/2 cotton produce a fabric with a suitable weight and hand for a jacket. Five colors are used in the warp and a single color, a gray-blue, is used for the thick weft, which ties the warp colors together and subdues them, keeping the jacket from being too gaudy. Choose other color blends to work with your wardrobe, using a medium-value coordinating thick weft.

❑ Equipment. 4-shaft loom, 30" weaving width (or width required by jacket pattern); 12-dent reed; 2 boat shuttles.

❑ Materials. Warp: 16/2 cotton (6700 yds/lb, Maurice Brassard et Fils), 4 oz each maroon (M), yellow (Y), and green (G); 3 oz each peach (P) and blue (B). Thin weft: 16/2 cotton, yellow (Y), 5 oz. Thick weft: 8/4 cotton (1680 yds/lb, Maurice Brassard et Fils), slate, 1 lb (the 8/4 cotton used in this fabric is a much softer fiber than the 8/4 often called carpet warp); sewing thread; jacket pattern (this is Vogue 8547 which is no longer available; many similar patterns can be used and/or adapted); notions required by pattern.

❑ Wind a warp of 1080 ends of 16/2 cotton 6 yds long in the following color order: [48G, 12P, 48Y, 12G, 48M, 12Y, 48B, 12M, 48P, 12B] 3x; end with 48G, 12P, 48Y, 12G, 48M, 12Y.

❑ Spread in a raddle and wind on a single warp beam at a density of 36 epi; center for 30" weaving width. Secure lease sticks for threading but note that the threads are not taken in the exact order in which they were wound on the warping board.

❑ Thread following the draft in *1*. In each thick/thin group, four threads of one color make up the thick thread, a single thread from the succeeding color is the thin. For example, for the first block, thread 4 ends of green in separate heddles on shaft 1 then thread 1 end of peach on shaft 3 and repeat 11x (12x total). For the second block, thread 4 ends of yellow in separate heddles on shaft 2 and 1 end of green on shaft 4 and repeat 11x (12x total). For the third block, thread 4 ends of maroon in separate heddles on shaft 3 and 1 end yellow on shaft 1 and repeat 11x (12x total), and continue. As you thread, thin warp ends in the succeeding color cross the threads that compose the thick as they come from the back beam to the heddles. Because tension is firm during weaving, these crossings present no problems; the threads line up well when they reach the heddles. The alternative of threading the exact order of the colors would be a very time-consuming process.

❑ Weave following the draft in *1* for the number of inches required by your pattern. Estimate about 15% take-up and shrinkage when calculating warp width and length. Use the slate 8/4 cotton as the thick weft and the yellow 16/2 cotton as the thin weft. (Note that the color of the thin weft is also important in its effect on overall color. Experiment with one or two different colors of thin weft if available in order to choose the one that brings the best results. Weave the blocks in A, B, C, D order alternating 16 picks thick weft and 16 picks thin weft for each block. Some sampling is advised to achieve the right beat. Examine the fabric on p. 47. Notice that as the thick weft passes behind the thick warp, some of its color peeks through. Aim to make the horizontal lines of color (and the lines created by the thin weft) the same distance apart as the distance between the thin warp threads and the vertical stripes of weft color peeking through between warp threads. If you beat the weft in firmly in order to make the lines of color disappear, the resulting fabric will be too firm.

❑ Finish by machine stitching raw fabric edges. Machine wash, warm water, normal cycle for 10 minutes. Steam press fabric on cotton setting.

❑ Cut out pattern pieces using a single layer of fabric (make any extra pattern pieces needed instead of cutting on the fold). Machine zigzag or serge all cut edges immediately to secure. Assemble and sew the jacket following pattern directions.

❑ For further exploration: Use this draft for wonderfully insulating and drapable wool fabrics. Use, for example, Harrisville Shetland, JaggerSpun Maine Line 8/2 wool, or other 7/2 or 8/2 wool doubled for the thick ends and picks. Use sewing thread or 20/2 or 30/2 cotton for the thin ends and picks. When this fabric is washed and slightly fulled, the thin threads virtually disappear, leaving a patterned cloth of squares of undiluted color. The reverse side of the fabric shows the opposite colors (thick warp on one side, thick weft on the other). Sley the wool at 1/dent in a 12-dent reed for 12 epi. Use two of the wool ends as one working end, 6 working thick ends/inch. Sley 1 thin end in every other dent (6 thin ends/inch). When designing fabrics for this draft, wind yarns on a ruler, leaving a tiny space between groups designated as one thick working end. The sett should be only very slightly more open than this wrap. Threads can be doubled or more for the thick weft also, but it makes easier weaving if the thick weft can be delivered in one pass. Consider using rayon chenille for the thick ends (2 working chenille ends/dent in an 8-dent reed). The thin ends bind the chenille securely. ✄

thick 'n thin tied weaves

beyond tied weaves

Do you have a difficult time finding enough shafts for more interesting patterning? Do you become tense about the impractical nature of some of the more fanciful drafts because the float lengths are too long? Does your weaving suffer from 'fear of floats'?

Seriously, tied weaves are a marvelous class of structures that can easily solve the float problem. With relatively few shafts, the weaver/designer can create patterns freely.

'Tied weaves' belong to the class of weaves featuring one warp and two wefts. The warp both creates a ground cloth with the ground weft and ties a supplementary weft to that cloth at regular intervals to limit float length. The supplementary weft shows on the face of the cloth in some places and on the back of the cloth in others to form the design.

TIED-WEAVE TERMINOLOGY

Tied weaves have been a subject of some confusion in weaving literature. As handweaver-researchers a generation ago discovered and re-discovered these systems for themselves, they often published their 'finds' with personal or descriptive names. They did the best they could, had fun with the naming, and went on, which has resulted in some mighty confused weavers in the next generation. What are 'Quigley,' 'Bergman,' and 'Landes Hybrid'? The name 'summer and winter' is poetic but hardly gives a clue to its structural nature.

Industrial texts avoid this whole problem but create another. In the textile industry, these weave structures are often called by the misnomer 'tapestry weaves.' This scarcely clears up the vocabulary question. Irene Emery, in *The Primary Structure of Fabrics,* defines the category as 'counterchanged extra-weft float weave' (p. 170). It isn't a pretty name, but it does describe the structure as long as you understand her terminology. Most handweavers today call these weaves 'tied' weaves. Tied weaves can be classified according to six variables: 1) ground weave structure, 2) frequency and number of ties in the threading, 3) lifting order of ties, 4) threading order of the pattern (non-tie) shafts, 5) lifting order of the pattern shafts, and 6) the ratio of ground picks to pattern picks.

Most of the conventional tied-weave structures in handweaving literature are unit weaves. Whether or not a tied weave is a unit weave is important if a block profile draft is to be used for the design, but not all of the possible threadings for tied weaves necessarily meet the requirements of a unit weave. (For an overview of tied weaves, unit weaves, and blocks see Doramay Keasbey, *Designing with Blocks for Handweavers*, 1993, and Madelyn van der Hoogt, *The Complete Book of Drafting for Handweavers*, 1993.)

Ground weave structure

Most of the common tied weaves produce a plain-weave ground cloth. No matter how they are threaded, Bergman, summer and winter, tied overshot, etc., all have a tabby weft that forms the fabric base. One can pull out the pattern weft and still have a viable plain-weave textile.

There are at least two reasons why a plain-weave ground may not always suit the needs of a textile: hand and color. There are occasions when the relatively stiff drape of a plain-weave fabric may be undesirable. The threading for the Peach Sherbet scarf, p. 54, produces a 3-shaft twill ground cloth. Three fine tie-down ends on shafts 1–3 are followed by a thick pattern thread. The softly drapable cloth has none of the 'boardy' qualities sometimes associated with plain-weave grounds. Twill or satin grounds can also add to the possibilities of playing with colors in the ground warp and weft. Unlike plain weave, which produces a relatively even pointillist blending of colors, twill can be warp-effect, weft-effect, or balanced, and it can show right- or left-handed diagonals.

Frequency and number of ties

The tie-down warp ends tie the supplementary pattern weft to the cloth at regular intervals on both faces of the fabric to relieve us of our 'fear of floats'! The genius of tied weaves is that the same warp threads that participate in creating the ground-weave structure also act to limit the length of the pattern-weft floats.

Tie-down threads can be threaded on two, three, or even more shafts to be referred to as 2-, 3-, or 4-tie weaves, etc. The greater the number of ties and/or the less frequently they are spaced, the longer the pattern floats become.

Summer and winter is a two-tie unit weave. Tie-down warp ends are threaded alternately on shafts 1 and 2. The tie down ends alternate with pattern ends, A = 1-3-2-3, B = 1-4-2-4; see the draft in *1*. The tied weaves described by Margaret Bergman are 3-tie weaves, and those described by Joyce Quigley

1. Summer and winter

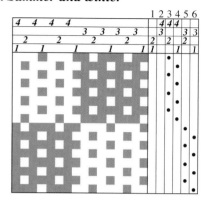

are 4-tie weaves. In them, as in summer and winter, the tie-down ends alternate with pattern ends. Three or four tie-down ends can be threaded in a variety of twill orders: A = 1-4-2-4-3-4 (three ties); or A = 1-4-3-4-2-4-1-4-3-4-1-4-2-4-3-4 (three ties); or A = 1-5-2-5-3-5-4-5 (four ties). In all of these, the ratio of tie-down ends to pattern ends is 1:1. Two-tie weaves such as 'Landes Hybrid' and 'half dukagang' increase the length of pattern-weft floats by increasing the number of pattern ends between each tie-down end. Paired-tie weaves place two tie-down ends next to each other in the threading followed by two or more pattern ends; see Jan Blesi, pp. 71–72.

Lifting order of the ties

The lifting order of the tie-down ends for the pattern picks creates a design within the blocks of pattern and background and gives tied weaves much of their special character. Merely saying that a draft is a 2- or 3-tie weave does not tell us what it really looks like, because the ties can be manipulated in many ways. The two ties in summer and winter, for example, can be raised in several different orders: alternately, in pairs, or singly to form columns. Other 2-tie weaves such as Landes Hybrid raise a single tie for a number of picks and then the other tie for the same number to make alternating columns.

The ties in 3- and 4-tie weaves can be lifted (as well as threaded) in a variety of twill orders, such as the rosepath threading and treadling orders of 3-tie Bergman. For the greatest definition of pattern areas on the face of the cloth in weaves with more than two ties, one tie shaft is usually raised at a time for the pattern picks; i.e., in 1/2 or 1/3 twill order, which shows the pattern weft over the maximum number of ends. The band of drawdowns across the top of pp. 52–53 shows some of the possibilities (left to right):

thin thick 'n thin thick 'n thin thick 'n thin thick 'n thin thick 'n thin thick 'n thin thick 'n thin thick 'n thin thick 'n thin thick 'n thin thick 'n thin thick 'n
thin thick 'n thin thick 'n thin thick 'n thin thick 'n thin thick 'n thin thick 'n thin thick 'n thin thick 'n thin thick 'n thin thick 'n thin thick 'n thin thick 'n
thick 'n thin thick 'n thin thick 'n thin thick 'n thin thick 'n thin thick 'n thin thick 'n thin thick 'n thin thick 'n thin thick 'n thin thick 'n thin thick
thick 'n thin thick 'n thin thick 'n thin thick 'n thin thick 'n thin thick 'n thin thick 'n thin thick 'n thin thick 'n thin thick 'n thin thick 'n thin th

Identifying the variables that go into any of these tied weaves illuminates the many ways that a textile designer can create extremely varied and exciting textiles.

The Macintosh vest is named after the Scottish architect and textile designer Charles Rennie Macintosh.

The curvy lines of the Flames scarf are created by threading the pattern shafts in an advancing twill order. The diversified plain weave draft for the vest (see p. 56) places thick and thin threads in both warp and weft.

ck 'n thin thick 'n thin thick 'n thin thick 'n thin thick 'n thin thick 'n thin thick 'n thin thick 'n thin thick 'n thin thick 'n thin thick 'n thin thick 'n thin thick
thin thick 'n thin thick 'n thin thick 'n thin thick 'n thin thick 'n thin thick 'n thin thick 'n thin thick 'n thin thick 'n thin thick 'n thin thick 'n thin thick 'n thin thic
ck 'n thin thick 'n thin thick 'n thin thick 'n thin thick 'n thin thick 'n thin thick 'n thin thick 'n thin thick 'n thin thick 'n thin thick 'n thin thick 'n thin thick 'n
k 'n thin thick 'n thin thick 'n thin thick 'n thin thick 'n thin thick 'n thin thick 'n thin thick 'n thin thick 'n thin thick 'n thin thick 'n thin thick 'n thin thi

Landes Hybrid, tied overshot, the paired-tie weave 'tied Lithuanian,' Bergman, half satin, Quigley with ties raised in broken-twill order, Quigley with ties raised in straight-twill order, and a 5-tie weave with ties raised in satin order.

Threading order of the pattern shafts

Traditionally weavers use tied weaves to produce block designs, in which units of one block are frequently repeated to create large areas of the same block. Conventional block designs combine large, medium, and small block sizes in both horizontal and vertical directions.

But these geometric, symmetrical designs are not the only alternative. Even when treating tied weaves as unit weaves, freer patterns are possible. One way is to thread single units of each block either in succession or in a variety of twill orders. The design in *2* shows blocks threaded in single-unit widths in a networked twill curve and an advancing point twill order.

For even smoother curves in the design, use partial units. With summer and winter, for example, one tie-down end can be threaded with a pattern shaft from one block, and the next tie-down end with a pattern shaft from a different block (A = 1, 3; B = 2, 4, etc.), as long as the tie-down ends alternate in the threading as usual. This same principle is true for all tied weaves: if, for example, the structure is Quigley and the four tie shafts are threaded in rosepath order, thread 1-P-2-P-3-P-4-P-1-P-4-P-3-P-2-P where each P is *any* pattern shaft required by the design. In the summer and winter draft in *3*, the pattern shafts are threaded (from right to left) in straight, point, networked, advancing, advancing point, undulating, and irregular twill orders. (Tabby picks are not shown in the drafts in *1–6*). More shafts and dobby treadling systems allow curvilinear images, such as the design for the summer-and-winter Flames scarf (p. 51) in *4*. The threading of the pattern shafts for the scarf is in an advancing point-twill order. (The draft in *4* shows only the threading and lifting orders of the pattern shafts; the threading of tie shafts and tabby picks are not shown.)

Straight and point sequences of blocks produce designs that are easy to visualize and are familiar to handweavers. Advancing twill orders of blocks are a bit more difficult to predict without actually drafting them. They modify a motif in two ways: by softening

the hard edges of the motif, and by increasing its width. The treadling sequence must be elongated to compensate for the added width of the advancing twill in the threading; note the elongated flames in the lifting order for the Flames scarf in *4*. Fine yarns tend to further minimize the blocky nature of the structure.

Lifting order of the pattern shafts

The beauty of tied weaves lies in their patterning possibilities. This is best illustrated by looking closely at the pattern section of a tie-up, particularly in a skeleton tie-up. A skeleton tie-up gives the weaver more pattern possibilities: instead of tying the tie shafts on the same treadles as the pattern shafts, the tie-shafts are tied to separate treadles and two treadles are depressed together. The weaver can then select the tie-down order independently of the pattern, and only one treadle is required for each pattern-shaft combination. Each square in the pattern section of the tie-up can be filled or left blank at will. Examine the sample tie-up for summer and winter in *5*. Two treadles are used for tabby and two for the tie-down shafts. The remaining can be used for pattern; a section six squares high and six squares wide, or 36 total squares can be filled in any way at all. Just a few possibilities are shown in *5*.

If your 8-shaft loom is a table loom or a dobby, your design area is six squares wide and infinitely high. Here you can let your imagination roam: waves, trees, animals, leaves, flowers, or abstracts. Are you having fun yet?

Ratio of ground picks to pattern picks

While ground picks alternate one-and-one with pattern picks in most tied weaves, this is not by any means the only option. Increasing the number of ground picks is usually not desirable, since the supplementary weft in most designs is meant to cover the ground. However, even here there are cases when the added security of two rows of ground or an emphasis upon lines in the weft direction may be called for.

If you increase the number of pattern-weft picks to two for every ground pick, you can use two different colors for the pattern weft and further enhance your design with shading, outlining, or illusions of depth. Summer and winter polychrome uses this technique; the two wefts in two different colors appear on the face of the cloth in different blocks.

There is no reason why some of the background cannot show as well.

What's next

By using these six variables you can create your own tied-weave structures without relying upon recipes. When you've mastered the basic principles, you'll be ready to add variables of fiber thickness and color to the mix!

Variations in fiber thickness

Variations in fiber thickness in both warp and weft are characteristic of the structure that has been called diversified plain weave in handweaving literature. In this weave, two thin threads surround each thick thread in both warp and weft; see pp. 8–11. If we extend that unwieldy terminology, the draft for the Peach Sherbet scarf, p. 54, should probably be called 'diversified twill'!

The draft for the Macintosh vest on p. 51, alternates one thin thread and one thick thread in both warp and weft (see p. 56) using a summer and winter threading and treadling system.

Whatever these structures are called, both the vest fabric and the scarf depends, as all tied weaves do, on the presence of regularly spaced tie-down threads that ensure an end to fear of floats! In the Peach Sherbet scarf, the ratio of three thin tie-down ends to one heavy pattern thread in both warp and weft gives it a unique texture and hand.

'n thin thick 'n thin thick 'n thin thick 'n thin thick 'n thin thick 'n thin thick 'n thin thick 'n thin thick 'n thin thick 'n thin thick 'n thin thick 'n
thin thick 'n thin thick 'n thin thick 'n thin thick 'n thin thick 'n thin thick 'n thin thick 'n thin thick 'n thin thick 'n thin thick 'n thin thick 'n
thick 'n thin thick 'n thin thick 'n thin thick 'n thin thick 'n thin thick 'n thin thick 'n thin thick 'n thin thick 'n thin thick 'n thin thick 'n thin thick 'n thin thick
thick 'n thin thick 'n thin thick 'n thin thick 'n thin thick 'n thin thick 'n thin thick 'n thin thick 'n thin thick 'n thin thick 'n thin thick 'n thin thick

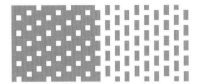
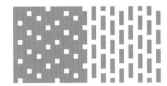
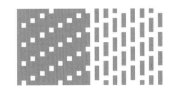
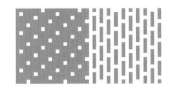

2. Summer and winter units threaded in twill orders

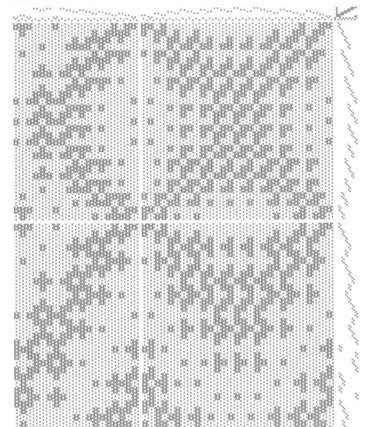

3. Partial units threaded in twill orders

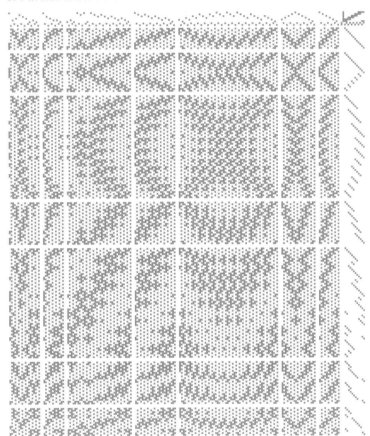

4. Threading for the Flames scarf

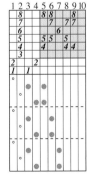

5. Designing 8-shaft tie-ups

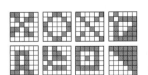

Fill in squares in the pattern section of the tie-up. To weave, depress a tie-down treadle with a pattern treadle for the pattern pick.

You can create your own tied-weave structures without relying upon recipes. Just be sure that your new creation takes each of the variables into account. So how many variations can we create? The number is staggering, even for an 8-shaft, 10-treadle loom. More shafts add options geometrically.

peach sherbet scarf

Use a scarf as a springboard to develop your own designs in this unusual version of a 3-tie weave—or is it 'diversified twill'? Whatever it's called, you'll love the drape created by the twill interlacement and the thick and thin threads.

"I have no business buying this warp," I said to the sales clerk in the Convergence booth. "I have so many yarns at home—I should dye them! But I just can't resist this gorgeous fiber and its ice-cream colors." This was the start of a scarf for a special colleague and friend. The directions that came with the warp suggested a 4-shaft twill—but of course I never weave anything the easy way. My pieces always push me to nudge the limits of whatever is my current weaving knowledge.

So evolved a fine twill ground that supports the ice-cream warp and softens the hand for the scarf. Since you probably won't be able to duplicate this warp exactly, use your scarf to experiment with the wonders of thick and thin yarns. Choose a thick fiber that is roughly 1000 yds/lb, or mix several thinner fibers together. If you discover that your fabric is too stiff, re-sley in an 8-dent reed, or if it is too loose, re-sley in a 12-dent reed.

- ❑ Equipment. 8-shaft loom, 10-dent reed, 2 shuttles.
- ❑ Materials. Thick warp: textured pre-wound warp from Hill Country Weavers (1701 South Congress, Austin, TX 78704, 512-707-7396), 126 ends, 2½ yds long in peach, mauve, pale pink, turquoise, violet, or equivalent thick fibers (1000–1400 yds/lb), approximately 4 oz total. Thin warp and weft: 30/2 wool (8400 yds/lb, Robin and Russ), dusty rose, 3½ oz. Thick weft: cotton chenille, (895 yds/lb, The Weaver's Place, 75 Mellor Ave., Cantonsville, MD 21288, 410-788-7262), white, 4 oz.
- ❑ Wind a thick warp of 126 ends, 2½ yds long; wind a separate thin warp of 391 ends 30/2 wool, 2½ yds long.
- ❑ Space the two warps together in a raddle, centered for 12"; beam together. Because the warp is so short, the take-up from the two different types of yarn is not different enough to cause tension problems. For longer warps, two warp beams or a system of weights are advised.
- ❑ Thread following the draft in *1*. Fine ends are threaded on shafts 1–3; thick ends are threaded on shafts 4–8.
- ❑ Sley 3 thin ends and 1 thick end in each dent of a 10-dent reed, 40 total epi; center for 12".
- ❑ Weave following selected treadling sequence in *1a–c* or experiment with other tie-up and treadling orders. For most of this scarf the thick pick is made using treadles 4–6, producing a warp effect on the back side of the scarf and a weft effect on the face. In random places, treadles 7–11 are used to produce subtle bands of warp-effect twill.
- ❑ Finish by removing from loom and securing ends with a twisted fringe (see p. 7). Handwash in warm water with mild liquid detergent or Orvus Paste. Lay flat to dry. Finished size is approximately 11" x 50". ✂

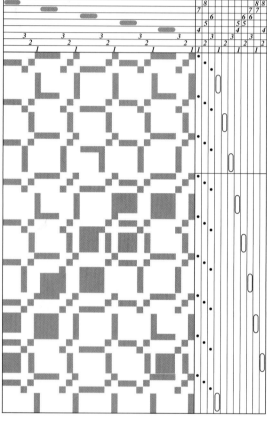

1a. Draft for scarf: diagonal design

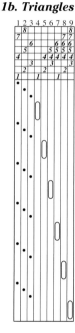

1b. Triangles

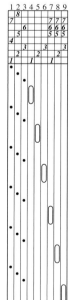

1c. Spots

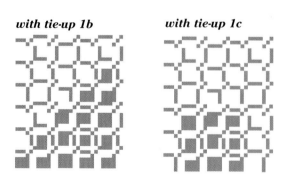

with tie-up 1b   *with tie-up 1c*

thin thick 'n thin thick 'n thin thick 'n thin thick 'n thin thick 'n thin thick 'n thin thick 'n thin thick 'n thin thick 'n thin
thin thick 'n thin thick 'n thin thick 'n thin thick 'n thin thick 'n thin thick 'n thin thick 'n thin thick 'n thin thick 'n
'n thin thick 'n thin thick 'n thin thick 'n thin thick 'n thin thick 'n thin thick 'n thin thick 'n thin thick 'n thin thick
thin thick 'n thin thick 'n thin thick 'n thin thick 'n thin thick 'n thin thick 'n thin thick 'n thin thick 'n thin thick 'n thin

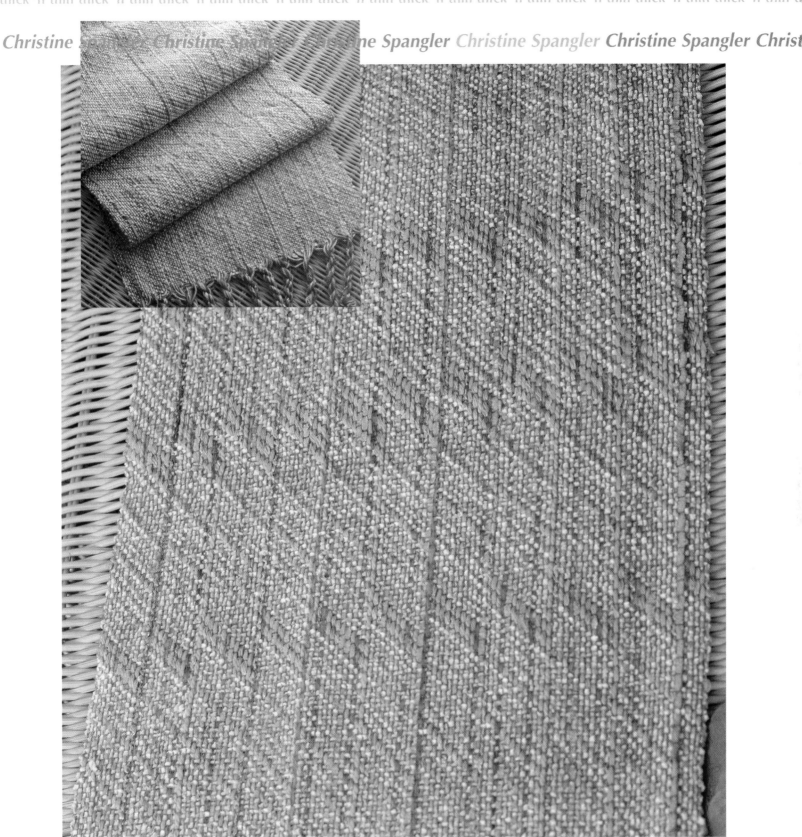

To vary the pattern in this scarf, try designing within the pattern section of the tie-up. Remember you are free to make any design at all without regard to the length of floats. Try other twill orders or lattice, spots, or triangle designs.

macintosh vest

1. Threading draft for Macintosh vest, p. 51

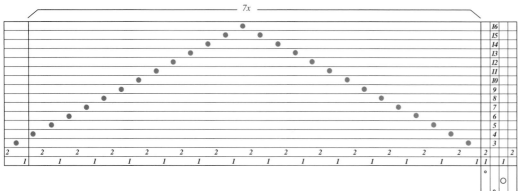

The pattern potential of thick 'n thin summer and winter can be enhanced by painting the fabric surface in selected places. The thick silk weft takes the acid dyes; the cotton threads do not. Since the design in this vest requires many different lifts, either a dobby or table loom must be used. Another option is to simplify the design; simpler flowers arranged in half drops (see 'Forty-five easy pieces,' pp. 57–60) are a good choice and can be woven using the number of treadles available on most 16-shaft looms.

- ❏ Equipment. 16-shaft dobby or table loom, 20" weaving width (check vest pattern for required width); 10-dent reed; 2 shuttles.
- ❏ Materials. Thick warp: 3/2 pearl cotton (1260 yd/lb), dark blue, 8¼ oz. Thin warp: 20/2 pearl cotton (8400 yds/lb), dark blue, 1¼ oz. Thick weft: #4 medium white singles silk (950 yd/lb, The Silk Tree), 9 oz. Pro Acid Washfast dyes in small amounts (.5% solution) for painting selected flowers (mixed to get green, orange, yellow, red, blue); vest pattern (this vest is small and the back is constructed from two pieces; adjust fabric amounts to pattern requirements).
- ❏ Wind a thick warp of 183 ends 3/2 cotton, 3½ yds long; wind a separate thin warp of 184 ends 20/2 cotton, 3½ yds long.
- ❏ Spread both warps in a raddle, centered for 18⅓"; beam together. If a difference in take-up between the two warps becomes a problem during weaving (the thick warp threads may become looser than the thin warp threads), raise shafts 1 and 2, slide a bar under these threads, and pass it over the back beam to hang below the warp beam. Suspend weights from this bar as necessary to add tension.
- ❏ Thread following the draft in *1*, thin 20/2 ends on shafts 1–2; thick 3/2 ends on shafts 3–16.

- ❏ Sley 1 thin end and 1 thick end in each dent of a 10-dent reed, 20 total epi; center for 18⅓".
- ❏ Derive a peg plan for the vest by adding tabby treadles and tie-down shaft lifts to the pattern profile in *2*. For example, a single treadling unit is shown in *3a*: a thin tabby pick, a pattern pick raising tie-down shaft 1, a thin tabby pick, and a pattern pick raising tie-down shaft 2. Any pattern shafts can be raised with shafts 1 or 2 for the pattern picks (blank in *3a*). *3b* shows the treadling for the first four pattern picks in *2* (read the profile from bottom to top; blue squares represent raised warp threads, orange and green squares represent the thick white weft after it is painted). The peg plan template corresponding to *3a* is shown in *4b*. Construct the full peg plan by adding pattern picks from *2* to the blank sections for the lifts of shafts 3–16 for the thick picks. Weave following the peg plan for 80".
- ❏ Finish by removing the fabric from the loom. Handwash in warm water with mild liquid detergent or Orvus Paste. Lay flat to dry. Finished fabric is approximately 17" x 72". Construct vest following pattern directions. ✂

2. Pattern profile

3. Deriving the treadles for first four pattern picks

4. Deriving the peg plan for first four pattern picks

forty-five easy pieces

"Linus Pauling, the Nobel Prize winning chemist, once said, 'The trick is to have lots of ideas and throw the bad ones away.' This method certainly led to excellence for him, so I try to follow it to improve my work as well."

I enjoy the process of designing complex-looking figurative patterns in simple structures—I never trust my first attempt. Like Dr. Pauling, only after I have explored several alternatives for a given design can I be satisfied that I have found the best solution.

Begin with a simple motif

To illustrate, we'll begin with a simple triangle motif, which is developed into a 6-block profile draft in *1*. Since rows of motifs lined up like toy soldiers are not my idea of an interesting design, let's try out some alternatives and discard the bad ones.

First, we'll add a square to the tie-up as in *2*. This single square causes the dark and light areas of the design to be visually balanced so that there is now some ambiguity as to which value is foreground and which background. This effect, known as 'counterchange,' makes the background just as active as the foreground. It avoids motifs that seem to float in space.

There are several other steps one can take to avoid toy soldiers: to vary the positions of the motifs in the rows, to change the scale of the design, and to blur the edges of the motif.

Half-drop the motif

First, to create more interest and break up the platoon, we can half-drop the motifs horizontally. In *3*, the motifs are offset from one another from row to row. The same effect can be achieved vertically as shown in *4*. When converted to a draft for weaving, the method in *3* requires more treadles, and the method in *4* more shafts. Note the characteristic diagonal that appears in the vertical half drop. Extra dots enliven the light areas and enhance the positive/negative ambiguity.

Next, let's flip the second row of triangles as in *5*. Flipping the image horizontally works especially well when combined with a horizontal half drop. Sometimes this makes it possible for the motifs to nest with each other, which helps to obscure the horizontal striping. These particular triangles do not lend themselves to nesting, however; see *6*.

1. Draft a motif

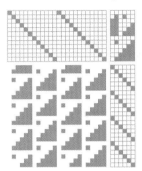

2. Add to the tie-up

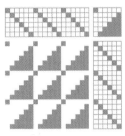

3. Horizontal half-drop

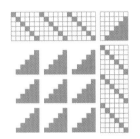

4.-Vertical half-drop

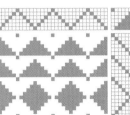

5. Flip alternate rows

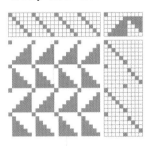

6. Nest the motifs

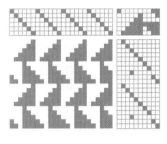

7. Mirror the threading

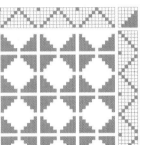

8. Mirror the treadling

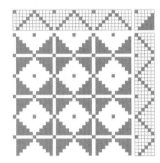

9. Add to the tie-up

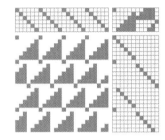

Mirror the motif

If you prefer the classical patterning of symmetrical balance, mirror the image along a vertical axis with a point threading as in *7*. Add a point treadling to mirror the image vertically. In *8*, the addition of two threads in each threading and treadling repeat separates the triangles with a grid. A square added to the tie-up in *8* enlivens the design in *9*.

Change the scale

Many of the designs in *1–9* are pleasing, but depending on the chosen weave structure and yarn size, their scale when woven may be quite small. Tiny patterns are excellent for apparel but are usually less desirable in wall hangings or liturgical, theater, or upholstery fabrics. The most obvious way to increase scale is to enlarge the block—vertically, horizontally, or both; see *10*, p. 58.

However, there are some other options that can increase the scale of the design while also avoiding a blocky look. As in all things, however, one gives up something to get something.

Soften motif edges

To avoid stair-stepping in large blocks, the motif edges must be softened, or blurred. This can be accomplished in several ways. The draft in *11* illustrates just two of them: blocks are threaded in a 3-end advancing twill order (1-2-3, 2-3-4, 3-4-5, etc.) and in a 4-end advancing twill order (1-2-3-4, 3-4-5-6, 5-6-1-2).

The top two treadlings in *11* are in straight order, each block combination is repeated three and then two times. The next treadling sequence begins with a 3-end advancing twill order and ends by repeating one block combination. The fourth and fifth sequenc-

ck 'n thin thick 'n thin thick 'n thin thick 'n thin thick 'n thin thick 'n thin thick 'n thin thick 'n thin thick 'n thin thick 'n thin
ck 'n thin thick 'n thin thick 'n thin thick 'n thin thick 'n thin thick 'n thin thick 'n thin thick 'n thin thick 'n thin thick 'n thin thic
thin thick 'n thin thick 'n thin thick 'n thin thick 'n thin thick 'n thin thick & thin thick 'n thin thick 'n thin thick 'n thin thick 'n
k 'n thin thick 'n thin thick 'n thin thick 'n thin thick 'n thin thick 'n thin thick 'n thin thick 'n thin thick 'n thin thick 'n thin thi
k 'n thin thick 'n thin thick 'n thin thick 'n thin thick 'n thin thick 'n thin thick 'n thin thick 'n thin thick 'n thin thic

10. Vary the scale of the motif

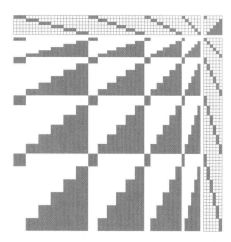

es use 3- and 4-end advancing twill orders. These effects provide counterchange between the light and dark areas and a fuzziness, or visually blended area, between the two values. From a distance, the pattern gives an illusion of depth, of shadows in boxes. This is especially true of the fourth and fifth treadling orders.

The next variation combines advancing point-twill threading orders with either advancing point-twill treadling or straight-twill treadling orders; see *12*. Our simple triangle has certainly gained a great deal more character!

If we take the threadings in *11* and mirror them horizontally and use straight, advancing, and mirrored treadlings, we add sixteen more designs to the collection; see *13*.

Finally, if the designs in *12* receive the same treatment, we add four more designs in *14* and bring the total to forty-five! These are by no means all the possibilities we can derive from the humble triangle. Other threading and treadling orders can be used or further minor changes can be made to the motif. One can also fine-tune the threadings and treadlings almost endlessly. But we have to stop somewhere!

From profile draft to weave structure

So now you say, "These designs are fine, but they are merely *profile* drafts. What do I *do* with them?" My prejudice toward figurative design is the reason I generally choose supplementary-weft structures with tie-down threads to produce the images. A two-tie unit weave such as summer and winter is one of the least expensive weaves in terms of shaft usage.

11. Advancing straight-twill order

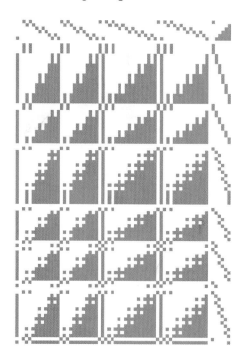

12. Advancing point-twill order

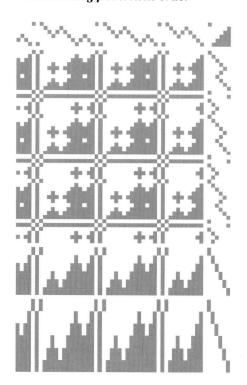

13. Mirrored advancing straight twill

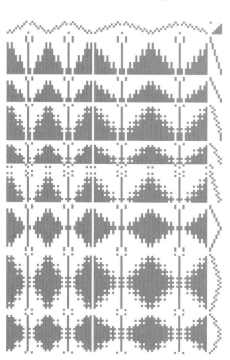

14. Mirrored advancing point twill

'n thin thick 'n thin thick 'n thin thick 'n thin thick 'n thin thick 'n thin thick 'n thin thick 'n thin thick 'n thin thick 'n thin thick 'n
thin thick 'n thin thick 'n thin thick 'n thin thick 'n thin thick 'n thin thick 'n thin thick 'n thin thick 'n thin thick 'n thin thick 'n
thick 'n thin thick 'n thin thick 'n thin thick 'n thin thick 'n thin thick 'n thin thick 'n thin thick 'n thin thick 'n thin thick 'n thin thick
thin thick 'n thin thick 'n thin thick 'n thin thick 'n thin thick 'n thin thick 'n thin thick 'n thin thick 'n thin thick 'n thin thick 'n thin t

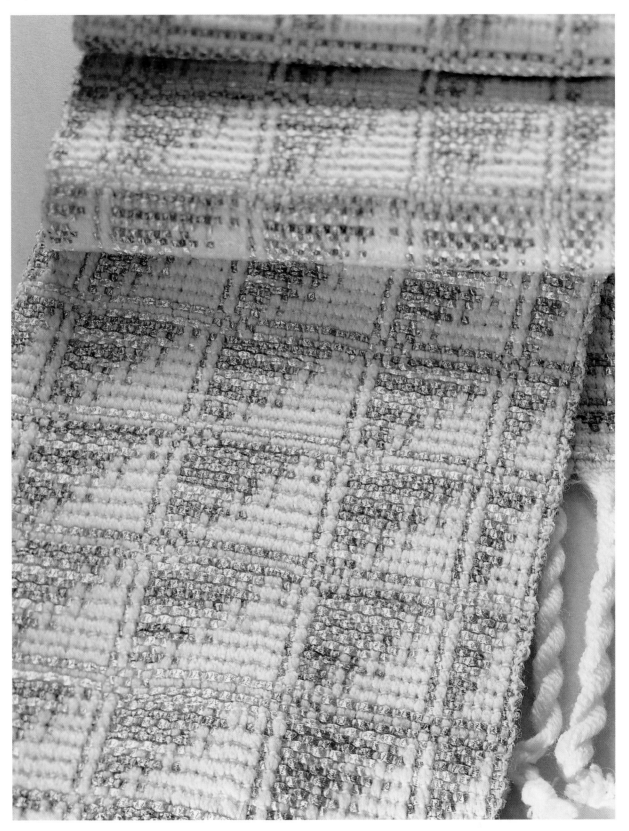

*The design for this scarf is only one of forty-five different designs derived from a simple triangle motif.
Learn the process and let your imagination roam: leaves, woodgrain, lilies, faces, curves, abstract
shapes, fractals, tessellations. Even the simplest motifs are rich with design potential.*

The two tie-down ends occupy the first two shafts; the rest are free for patterning. Each additional shaft provides a block of pattern. Thus for the average 8-shaft, 10-treadle loom, one can design with up to six different blocks in the horizontal direction and eight block combinations vertically. Table or dobby looms add complete freedom to the number of block combinations in the vertical direction.

Summer and winter half units

The summer-and-winter structural unit consists of four threads: Block A = 1-3-2-3; Block B = 1-4-2-4; Block C = 1-5-2-5, etc. Usually, the four ends of one structural unit are considered the minimum number of threads that can be assigned to a particular block. However, the unit can be split so that the minimum number for a block is one tie-down end and one pattern end. The only restriction is that shafts 1 and 2 must always alternate with each other between pattern ends: 1, P1, 2, P2, 1, P3, 2, P4, etc. The pattern threads can be threaded on *any* of the other shafts (3 through the highest number on your loom) in *any* order.

Enhance the design with thick threads in warp and weft

A thread-by-thread summer-and-winter drawdown for the triangles in *1* (p. 57) is shown in *15a*. Note that one pattern thread (with its accompanying tie-down end) represents a block: Block A on shaft 3, Block B on shaft 4, etc. The profile draft in *1* is merely copied on rows 3–8, the tie-down ends placed in between.

Because the summer-and-winter drawdown does not distinguish between the size of the tabby weft and the size of the pattern weft, the pattern is indistinct. The drawdown, in fact, looks like a cloth would look in which the tabby weft and pattern weft are the same size. To increase the role of the pattern threads in both warp and weft directions (rather than only in the weft direction as in traditional summer and winter), use thick (or multiple) ends for the pattern threads in both warp and weft. Compare the drawdowns in *15a* and *15b* to see how the thicker threads enhance the pattern and obscure the structure.

A portion of the draft in *11* is used as the basis for the draft for the Shadow Box scarf; see p. 61. Straight threading and treadling orders of the blocks are added at the sides and at the top and bottom of the scarf to frame the larger triangles. The advancing-twill order in threading and treadling directions enlarges the motif. For this scarf, treadling 'as-drawn-in' automatically squares the pattern.

15a. Summer and winter draft

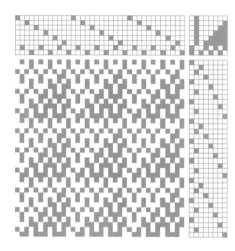

15b. Thick threads in warp and weft ❏

Scarf fabric uses thick threads in both warp and weft.

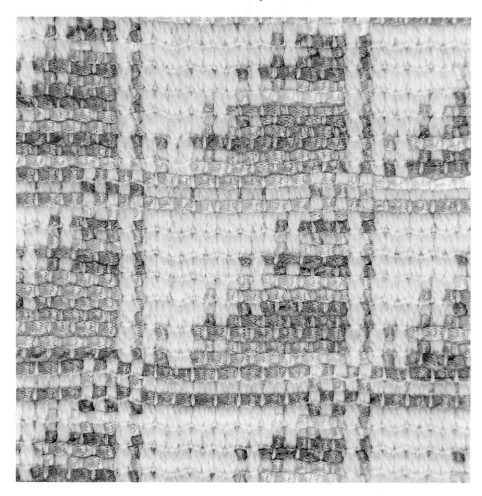

thin thick 'n thin thick 'n thin thick 'n thin thick 'n thin thick 'n thin thick 'n thin thick 'n thin thick 'n t
in thick 'n thin thick 'n thin thick 'n thin thick 'n thin thick 'n thin thick 'n thin thick 'n thin thick 'n t
'n thin thick 'n thin thick 'n thin thick 'n thin thick 'n thin thick 'n thin thick 'n thin thick
ick 'n thin thick 'n thin thick 'n thin thick 'n thin thick 'n thin thick 'n thin thick 'n thin th

16a. 8-shaft draft for Shadow Box scarf

																														1 2 3 4 5 6 7 8					

- 20/2 wool • ribbon

Thread a—e 1x, d—e 2x, b—c 1x (20/2 wool on shafts 1—2, 8/2 wool on shafts 3—8). Thread 2 ends 20/2 wool on shafts 1 and 2 at each selvedge. Weave a—e 1x, d—e for 58—60", b—c 1x.

16b. 4-shaft draft for Shadow Box scarf

Thread 20/2 wool on shafts 1—2, 8/2 wool on shafts 3—4. Weave a—b 1x, b—c for 58—60", c—d 1x.

17a. Profile draft for 8-shaft Shadow Box scarf

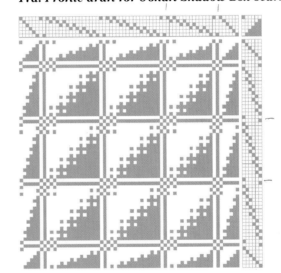

17b. Profile draft for 4-shaft Shadow Box scarf

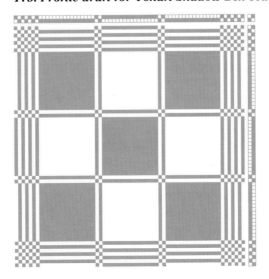

dark/
hoose
width;

Maine
p and
Snow,
(The
e, MD
21288, 410-788-7262), green/pink space-dyed color #9004, two 50-gram balls.

❏ Wind a warp of 132 thick (66 doubled 8/2 ends) and 70 thin (20/2) ends, 2½ yds long in the following order: 2 thin, [1 thin, 2 thick]66x, 2 thin.

❏ Sley 1 thin and 2 thick ends in each dent of an 8-dent reed (sley the 2 thin edge threads in the same dent on each side), 24 total epi; center for 8½".

❏ Thread according to the draft in *16a*: a–e 1x, d–e 2x, b–c 1x, or thread according to the 4-shaft draft in *16b*. Thin ends are threaded on shafts 1 and 2; thick ends are threaded on shafts 3–8 (3–4 in *16b*). Two thick ends are threaded together in each heddle on shaft 3 and above.

❏ Weave following the treadling sequence in *16a*: a–e 1x, d–e for desired length of the scarf (62"–64"), b–c 1x. Follow the treadling in *16b* for the 4-shaft draft a–b 1x, b–c for 58–60", c–d 1x. Allow 8" each end for fringe. Weave with moderate tension on the warp. Flatten each shot of the thick weft ribbon as you weave.

❏ Finish by removing from the loom and securing the ends with a twisted fringe: Starting at one edge, separate two groups of fringe consisting of 3 doubled thick/3 thin ends each. Twist the two groups together in the same direction until they kink. Then twist both groups together in the opposite direction and secure with an overhand knot. Handwash the scarf in warm water with Orvus Paste or a mild soap. Lay flat to dry. The finished size of the scarf is approximately 8" x 60". ✄

For a lovely spring scarf, use thick pattern threads in both the warp and the weft to intensify the design and soften summer and winter's usually busy, speckled look. The contrast between pattern and background is intensified by the contrast between the shiny rainbow-colored ribbon and soft white wool.

reach for the stars

Laura Fry Laura Fry Laura Fry Laura Fry Laura Fry Laura Fry Laura Fry **Laura Fry** Laura Fry Laura Fry Lau

1. Threading draft for jacket

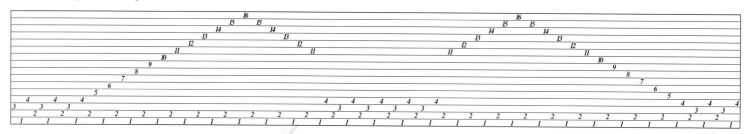

Thick threads in soft-spun silk alternate with very thin threads in both warp and weft to produce the subtle stars in this jacket. The thin threads weave an invisible frame for the thick threads. Pattern is formed where thick warp threads are held up for a thick pick; background occurs where the thick weft threads show. Since a single thick thread constitutes one pattern block, motifs with finer definition (like these delicate stars) can be formed than with a traditional 4-thread summer and winter unit.

SILK JACKET
in thick 'n thin summer & winter

❑ Equipment. 16-shaft dobby loom, 48" weaving width; 10-dent reed; 2 boat shuttles.
❑ Materials. Thick warp (shafts 3–16): 30/2 silk (7500 yds/lb, Treenway Silks), dyed in variegated blue violet to red violet tones, ⅔ lb (each dyed skein is either predominantly red violet or blue violet). Thin warp (shafts 1–2): 120/2 silk (49,500 yds/lb), white, 2 oz. Thick weft: 30/2 silk, white, ⅔ lb. Thin weft: 2-ply silk (40,000 yds/lb, Craft Cottage, Richmond, B.C.), one ply royal blue, one ply orange, 2 oz; jacket pattern, lining, notions required by pattern.
❑ Wind a warp of 963 ends (wind one thick and one thin end together on the warping board, keeping the strands separate with a finger; end with an extra thin end) 5 yds long. For this jacket, the thick warp changes from blue violet to red violet: Starting at the right selvedge, use only blue violet. After 12", add red violet ends gradually until until all ends are red violet at the left selvedge.
❑ Sley 2/dent in a 10-dent reed (1 thick end, 1 thin end in each dent), 20 epi; center for 48".
❑ Thread following the draft in *1* 9x. Add 1 floating selvedge of 120/2 silk to each side.
❑ Weave following the treadling sequence in *2* or the peg plan in *3*. Note that the treadling and peg plan sequences reverse at both top and bottom (do not repeat sheds at reversal points). Use white 30/2 silk for thick weft, fine royal/orange silk for thin weft. If thin ends break at the selvedges, substitute a heavier fiber such as 20/2 cotton for the last two 120/2 ends on each side.
❑ To finish, serge raw ends. Machine wash with detergent in warm water. (Optional: A cup of vinegar in the final rinse water adds crunch to the silk.) Machine dry, gentle, until just damp; steam press. (Tumbling the silk softens it. If allowed to air dry, the fabric tends to be stiff.) Allow for about 10% shrinkage.
❑ Cut and assemble following jacket pattern. For this jacket, the pattern is placed carefully so that one sleeve is blue violet, and the other is red violet. The fabric of the body of the jacket shades from blue violet to red violet. ✂

2. Treadling sequence for jacket

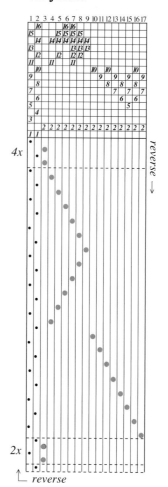

3. Peg plan for jacket

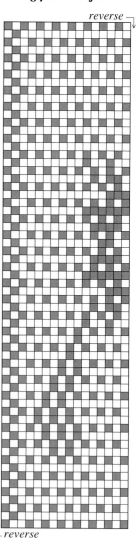

thick 'n thin thick 'n th

Laura Fry Laura Fry Laura Fry Laura Fry Laura Fry Laura Fry Laura Fry Laura Fry Laura Fry Laura Fry Laura Fry La

glowing crosses runner

Jo Anne Ryeburn Jo Anne Ryeburn Jo Anne Ryeburn Jo Anne Ryeburn Jo Anne Ryeburn Jo Anne Ryeb

1. Draft for Glowing Crosses runner

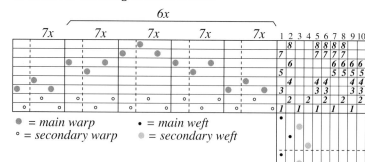

● = *main warp*   • = *main weft*
○ = *secondary warp*   ● = *secondary weft*

Warm, bright windows of color contrast with a cool background in this runner. Play with color sequences but be sure that the color of the thick warp blends with the color of the thin weft and vice versa. If the thin warp is a neutral color, many thick weft colors can be used effectively.

In this thick 'n thin version of lampas, warp-faced patterning in one colorway shows against a weft-faced background in a contrasting colorway. Thick main weave warp threads weave with a thin main weft; thick secondary weft threads weave with a thin secondary warp; see the draft in *1*. The thick threads therefore predominate in both pattern and background areas. (See Betsy Blumenthal, pp. 101–103.)

The draft in *1* produces a 'stitched' (also called 'integrated') version of lampas. Leaving the pattern blocks unstitched results in the deflection of the threads and sleazy pattern areas. An added bonus of this version of 'stitched' lampas is that it is reversible; pattern and background colors trade places on the reverse sides of the fabric.

❑ Equipment. 8-shaft loom, 19" weaving width; 10-dent or 20-dent reed; 2 shuttles.
❑ Materials. Amounts produce one runner 50" long. For a longer runner or more pieces, add to amounts and warp length. Take-up is about 10%.

Secondary (thin) warp: 20/2 mercerized cotton (8400 yds/lb, Durene, Robin and Russ) dyed with fiber-reactive dye according to Dye Chart Color f or 20/2 pearl cotton (8400 yds/lb, Halcyon, item #85) color #122, dark purple, 2 oz.
Main (thick) warp (five colors): 10/2 mercerized cotton (4200 yds/lb, Durene, Robin and Russ) dyed with fiber-reactive dyes, Dye Chart Colors a–e, or 10/2 pearl cotton (4200 yds/lb, Halcyon, item #84):
Color a (or Halcyon color #121, garnet), 1 oz;
Color b (or Halcyon color #120, dark red), 1 oz;
Color c (or Halcyon color #148, red orange), 1 oz;
Color d (or Halcyon color #146, orange), 1 oz;
Color e (or Halcyon color #145, light orange), ⅛ oz.
Main (thin) weft: 20/2 mercerized cotton (8400 yds/lb, Durene, Robin and Russ), Dye Chart Color g, or 20/2 pearl cotton (8400 yds/lb, Halcyon, item #85) color #120, dark red, 1½ oz.
Secondary (thick) weft: 10/2 mercerized cotton, (4200 yds/lb, Durene, Robin and Russ), Dye Chart Color f, or 10/2 pearl cotton (4200 yds/lb, Halcyon, item #84) color #122, dark purple, 2½ oz.

❑ Dye fibers (if not using commercial yarns) according to Dye Chart. Depth of shade (DOS) is 1% for all threads if using Fibracron fiber-reactive dyes, 2% if using Procion MX fiber-reactive dyes.
❑ Wind a warp of 750 ends, alternating one 20/2 end with one 10/2 end (375 ends of each size thread) 2½ yds long in color order: [Color a 20, b 15, c 13, d 21, e 5, d 7, c 17, b 16, a 6]3x; end with 15 Color a.
❑ Sley 4/dent in a 10-dent reed or 2/dent in a 20-dent reed, 40 epi; center for 18¾".
❑ Thread following the draft in *1*.
❑ Weave a 2" header with scrap material. Weave a sufficient amount to allow for hemstitching; hemstitch. Continue weaving following treadling sequence in *1*, alternating thin and thick wefts until runner is approximately 54" long or length desired, ending with a solid background stripe. Hemstitch this edge as at the beginning.
❑ Finish by removing the runner from the loom; wash by hand in lukewarm water with Orvus Paste or mild liquid detergent. Rinse; squeeze water out in towel; lay flat to dry; steam press. Finished length is 50". ✂

DYE CHART

Color	Red	Navy	Gold
a	80%	20%	
b	95%	5%	
c	70%		30%
d	20%		80%
e	4%		96%
f	70%	30%	
g	90%	10%	

thin thick 'n thin thick 'n thin thick 'n thin thick 'n thin thick 'n thin thick 'n thin thick 'n thin thick 'n thin thick 'n thin thick 'n thin thick 'n
thin thick 'n thin thick 'n thin thick 'n thin thick 'n thin thick 'n thin thick 'n thin thick 'n thin thick 'n thin thick 'n thin thick 'n thin thick 'n
thick 'n thin thick 'n thin thick 'n thin thick 'n thin thick 'n thin thick 'n thin thick 'n thin thick 'n thin thick 'n thin thick 'n thin thick 'n thin thick
thin thick 'n thin thick 'n thin thick 'n thin thick 'n thin thick 'n thin thick 'n thin thick 'n thin thick 'n thin thick 'n thin thick 'n thin t

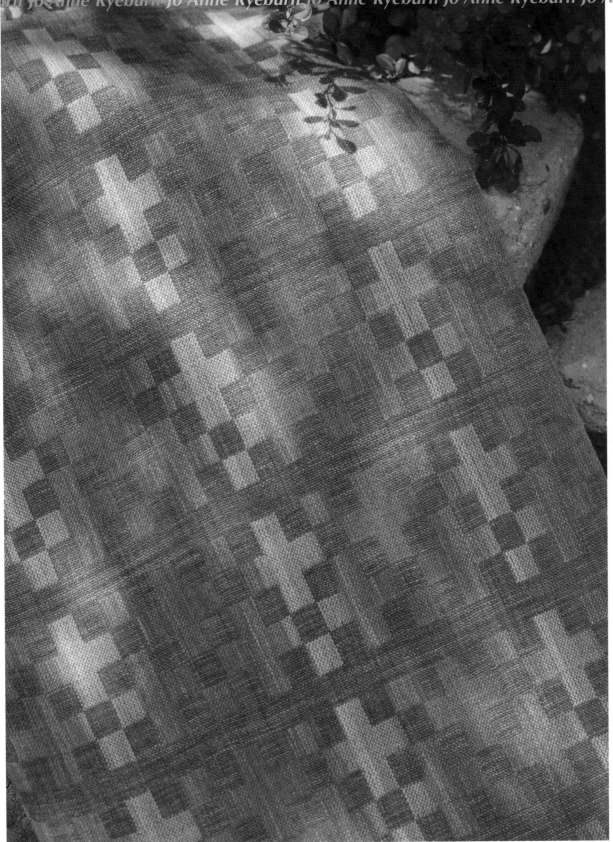

the incredible five-color afghan for a

David Xenakis David Xenakis David Xenakis David Xenakis David Xenakis **David Xenakis** David Xenak.

The afghan for a super kid is woven in three panels, each of which is 17" x 60". Two of the panels extend the pattern weft beyond the selvedge to make a sumptuous side fringe so that all four sides of the afghan are fringed.

After the three panels are woven, they are easily stitched together to give a final size of 50" x 60" (excluding fringe) to help keep your super kid warm on cold winter evenings.

There is a little treat for you, too (besides the weaving). This afghan is really durable! Your super kid can drag it off to college—it will tag along into adult relationships and still be in wonderful shape to keep warm a subsequent generation of super kids!

For best results, weave this afghan on a loom with two warp beams. If you have only one beam, suspend one of the warps from the back beam and weight.

1. Draft for afghan

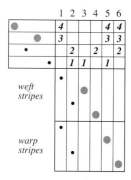

Numbers indicate number of times to weave repeats of the 4-pick weft stripe or warp stripes sequence; letters indicate color of thick weft (B=black, G=dark green, T=teal, R=dark red, O=orange). Thin weft is black throughout.

Weft stripes: 5B, 4R, 4T, 4G, 5B.
Warp stripes: 5B, 4G, 4T, 4R, 10B, 4O, 4G, 4O, 10B, 4R, 4T, 4G, 10B.
Weft stripes: 5B, 4G, 4T, 4R, 10B, 4O, 4G, 4O, 10B, 4R, 4T, 4G, 10B.
Warp stripes: 5B, 4G, 4T, 4R, 10B, 4O, 4G, 4O, 10B, 4R, 4T, 4G, 10B.
Weft stripes: 5B, 4G, 4T, 4R, 5B.

□ Equipment. 4-shaft loom, 18–32" weaving width for three panels (32" weaving width allows side fringe), 2 warp beams (optional but preferred); 6-dent reed (a 12-dent reed can be substituted but slight abrasion of thick warp will occur); 1 boat shuttle for thin weft, 5 stick shuttles for thick weft.

□ Materials. Thin warp and weft: 8/2 wool (2240 yd/lb, Maine Line, JaggerSpun), black, 14 oz. Thick warp and weft: 2-ply wool (392 yd/lb, Bulky, Brown Sheep), black (B) #210, 32 oz (8 skeins); dark green (G) #330, 12 oz (3 skeins); teal (T) #310, 8 oz (2 skeins), dark red (R) #200, 8 oz (2 skeins); orange (O) #232, 8 oz (2 skeins); a blunt-point stole weaving needle (Boye Needle Co., item No. 7517).

□ Wind a warp of 102 ends 8/2 wool 9 yds long. Wind a separate warp of 2-ply Bulky 9 yds long: 8B, 6G, 6T, 6R, 16B, 6O, 6G, 6O, 16B, 6R, 6T, 6G, 8B.

□ Sley the Bulky wool 1/dent in a 6-dent reed; center for 17". To thread, leave one empty heddle on shaft 1, thread one end on shaft 3, leave one empty heddle on shaft 2, thread one end on shaft 4; repeat.

□ Beam the 2-ply warp on the warp beam that is closest to the shafts (or on a single beam if you only have one) and tie onto the front apron rod to secure for the threading and beaming of the second (8/2) warp.

□ Place a strip of white cardboard 2" x 20" on top of the thick warp in front of the reed. Sley the 8/2 warp 1/dent in the same dents that have already been sleyed with the thick warp.

□ Thread the 8/2 ends through the empty heddles (skipped when threading the thick warp) alternately on shafts 1 and 2, and beam this warp on the second beam (or suspend from the back of the loom in eight 2⅛" chains and add weights to equal the tension of the Bulky warp). Remove cardboard strip; tie the 8/2 warp onto the front apron rod.

□ Weave a short heading in scrap yarn using treadles 1 and 2. Allow 7" warp length for fringe. Before beginning to weave the body of the first panel, add a floating selvedge of 8/2 black to the left side. Tie a heavy cord between the breast beam and the back beam on the right side in the same way as the floating selvedge but about 7" to the right of the warp. Use this cord as a guide for the weft fringe of the first panel. Begin the thick weft by loosely tying it to this cord. Pass the shuttle from right to left for the first thick pick. For the next thick pick, pass the shuttle around the floating selvedge and through the shed from left to right. Then pass the

shuttle around the guide cord before re-entering the next shed for the thick weft. The result will be a loop of pattern weft protruding from the right selvedge around the cord. Cut these loops of weft as the warp is advanced. The thin (8/2) weft does not pass around this cord, but weaves a normal selvedge. When weaving the center panel, remove the cord and add a floating selvedge of 8/2 black to the right side. When weaving the third panel, remove the floating selvedge from the left side and tie the guide cord 7" to the left of the warp to use for fringe along the left side.

□ Weave each of the three panels of the afghan following the directions in *1* (the center panel is turned over before seaming to join warp strip sections with weft stripe sections for the checked afghan design). The weft stripe sequence and the warp stripe sequence are each repeated a designated number of times with a designated color for the thick weft (for example, in *1*, 'weft stripes: 5B' means to weave the weft sequence 5 times with the black thick weft). Black is used as the thin weft throughout. End with a thin pick using treadle 1.

□ You can remove each panel from the loom as it is finished. Allow 7" for fringe on each end.

□ When all three panels are removed from the loom, lay the first on the table right side up. Use the point of the blunt needle to free the first thin (8/2) warp thread from the scrap yarn up to the beginning of the afghan. Thread it into the needle and darn the end back into the fabric along the path of the adjacent heavy warp thread for 2–3" to secure. Free the next thin warp end and darn it. Continue for all thin ends, leaving the darned-in ends protruding from the fabric until after the afghan is washed. Take care that the darned-in warp thread encircles the last thin (8/2) weft at each end.

□ Use a doubled strand of 8/2 wool and lace the panels together by stitching through alternate selvedge loops of the thick weft (turn the center panel so that the underside during weaving is the top side when seaming). When 8–10 loops have been laced together, pull the lacing thread taut, taking care not to gather the fabrics.

□ When the pieces have been joined, machine wash in cool water, mild soap, minimum agitation. Rinse thoroughly and spin to remove excess water. Lay flat to dry. Comb out and straighten the fringes while the wool is still damp. When dry, trim the fringes evenly and cut all protruding ends of yarn flush with the surface of the weaving. ✄

super kid

THE PRAIRIE WOOL COMPANION

November 1981   PREMIERE ISSUE $3.50

Large groups of warp and weft stripes alternate to produce a large, richly colored checked design that disguises the seams that join the three panels. Weave this ample piece on a 4-shaft loom as narrow as 18".

the mystery weave

Louisa Chadwick Louisa Chadwick Louisa Chadwick Louisa Chadwick Louisa Chadwick Louisa Chadwick Louisa Chadwick Louisa Chadwick Louisa Chadwi

"It all began with a version of parallel shadow weave based on a crackle threading system devised by Kim Marie Bunke; see pp. 74–78. In Kim's version, 3-thread warp floats make pattern; thick and thin threads are used in both warp and weft. With a rearrangement of her threading and some experimenting, it becomes a structure that can plug into any profile draft and weave pattern or background in any block independently of the others."

The resulting weave structure produces a very sturdy fabric perfect for upholstery, mats, runners, tote bags, vests, and jackets.

MYSTERY WEAVE BASICS

There are two basic options for threading this structure from a profile draft. In both versions two shafts are threaded for each block; thin warp ends in one color on one of the shafts, heavier warp threads in a contrasting color on the other. Two fiber sizes and colors are also used in the weft: a thin pick in a color similar to the thick warp threads, a thick pick in a color similar to the thin warp threads.

The unbalanced draft

The first version can be treated as a unit weave. A 'unit' consists of four warp ends (thin threads on odd shafts, thick threads on even shafts) and four weft picks. A half unit can be threaded and treadled as long as the odd/even alternation is maintained. This threading produces an unbalanced draft; in the resulting cloth, however, 2-thread floats appear on one side of each block.

The balanced draft

When the draft is balanced, the 2-thread floats occur symmetrically. Blocks contain an even number of threads except turning blocks, which have an odd number of threads, and descending blocks show a reversed shaft order from ascending blocks. To provide the symmetry, a thin warp thread is added to ∧ turning blocks, and a thin warp thread is subtracted for ∨ turning blocks as shown in *2*.

The 4-pick treadling sequence is the same for both versions. Odd shafts (thin threads) are raised for the blocks showing the color of the thick weft and even shafts (thick threads) for the shafts

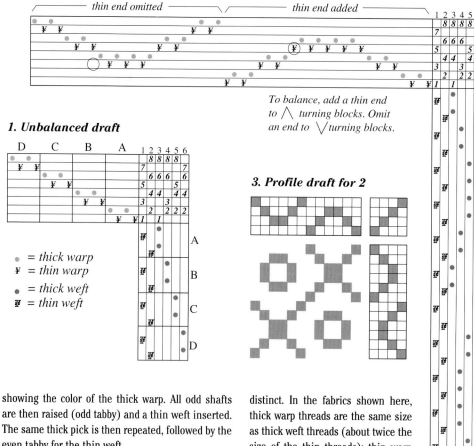

2. Balanced draft

thin end omitted — thin end added

To balance, add a thin end to ∧ turning blocks. Omit an end to ∨ turning blocks.

1. Unbalanced draft

= thick warp
¥ = thin warp
= thick weft
¥ = thin weft

3. Profile draft for 2

showing the color of the thick warp. All odd shafts are then raised (odd tabby) and a thin weft inserted. The same thick pick is then repeated, followed by the even tabby for the thin weft.

Mystery weave advantages

Blocks can be threaded and woven in any order and combined at will. Large-scale motifs can be designed without producing undesirable floats. Only two shafts are required per block and only one treadle for each block combination. Areas of all-pattern (all thick weft color) or all-background (all thick warp color) can be woven without separate treadles.

Special considerations

Yarns must be chosen carefully since both thickness and color influence the resulting cloth. The structure presents exciting options for color interaction. For best effects, thin thread warp threads should blend in value with the thick weft. The thick warp threads can consist of one, two, or many strands of similar values, but they should contrast with the pattern weft or the design will be obscured. Thin weft threads should blend with the colors of thick warp threads.

This structure can be woven with all warp and weft threads the same size, but the designs are then less

distinct. In the fabrics shown here, thick warp threads are the same size as thick weft threads (about twice the size of the thin threads); thin warp threads are the same size as the thin weft threads (except for the placemats, in which the thin weft is thicker than the thin warp to add density).

The sett should be fairly close so that the thick warp threads cover the pattern block; sampling is very important. The thick and thin warp threads can be beamed together without tension problems. Floating selvedges are mandatory.

Because pattern blocks overlap by one thread and the colors in pattern and background areas are so mixed, it is difficult to determine when a motif is squared. Warp take-up and shrinkage is greater than weft draw-in and shrinkage (weft take-up is minimal). To compensate, weave the motifs slightly longer than square. Allow extra warp for sampling to establish the correct beat, and measure with the tension as relaxed as possible.

Fabric drape is more pronounced horizontally. Cut garment pieces sideways to take better advantage of the direction of the drape. This also turns the pattern bars so that they produce flattering vertical lines.

thin thick 'n thin thick 'n thin thick 'n thin thick 'n thin thick 'n thin thick 'n thin thick 'n thin thick 'n thin thick 'r
thin thick 'n thin thick 'n thin thick 'n thin thick 'n thin thick 'n thin thick 'n thin thick 'n thin thick 'n thin thick 'n
k 'n thin thick 'n thin thick 'n thin thick 'n thin thick 'n thin thick 'n thin thick 'n thin thick 'n thin thick 'n thin thick
thin 'n thin thick 'n thin thick 'n thin thick 'n thin thick 'n thin thick 'n thin thick 'n thin thick 'n thin thick 'n thin t

Louisa's mystery weave provides the sturdy fabric for this vest. Rainbow colors in the warp are intensified by the navy pattern weft and thin black warp threads. A relative of diversified plain weave, this unusual structure invites experimentation with fiber color and thickness.

Warp and weft colors and a profile draft from Mary Atwater give a country quilt-like look to these placemats. With this weave, use any four-block profile draft on eight shafts for sturdy, durable fabrics suitable for upholstery, table linens, jackets, vests, coats, and totes.

4. Draft for vest

5. Draft for placemats

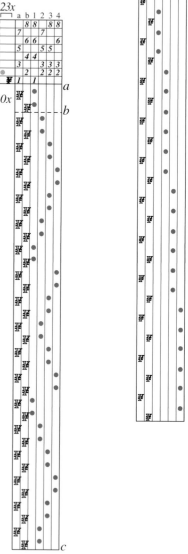

MYSTERY WEAVE VEST AND PLACEMATS

For the vest fabric, two blocks always weave together: AB, BC, CD, DA. In some of the blocks, thick threads are placed on odd shafts, thin on even; compare the threading for Block A in the center motif with Block A on the left and right sides of the motif. These blocks will always weave opposite from each other; where one shows the thick warp with a given treadle, the other will show the thick weft, adding further to design complexity.

❏ Equipment. 8-shaft loom, 30" weaving width; 12-dent reed; 2 shuttles.

❏ Materials. Thick warp: 8/2 unmercerized cotton (3600 yds/lb), 14 medium-value rainbow colors, about 5 oz total. Thin warp: 16/2 unmercerized cotton (6720 yds/lb), black, 3 oz. Thick weft: slub cotton (3,000 yds/lb), navy, ½ lb. Thin weft: 16/2 unmercerized cotton, medium gray, 3 oz. Vest pattern, navy cotton broadcloth for lining, matching sewing thread, 5 buttons.

❏ Wind a warp of 340 ends 8/2 cotton in rainbow color order (1 end each color) 3 yds long. Wind a separate warp of 341 ends 16/2 black cotton 3 yds long.

❏ Sley one 8/2 and one 16/2 end in each dent of a 12-dent reed, 24 epi; center for 28½".

❏ Thread following the draft in *4* beginning with a 16/2 end and alternating 16/2 and 8/2 ends throughout. Add one 16/2 end to each side for floating selvedges.

❏ Weave following draft at about 30 ppi (a bit weft-faced) for about 80" (measured with tension relaxed), which finishes to approximately 2 yds of 25¾" wide fabric—plenty for most vest patterns.

❏ Finish by securing raw edges with straight machine stitching. Machine wash, gentle, with regular detergent; air dry on padded clothesline; press with a hot iron. Cut and sew vest following pattern directions. Place pattern pieces carefully to line up motifs.

These mats are derived from a 4-block profile draft (#187) from Mary Atwater's Shuttle-Craft Book of American Hand-Weaving. *The design resembles quilt blocks to give the mats a country look. The draft is not balanced.*

❏ Equipment. 8-shaft loom, 16" weaving width; 12-dent reed; 2 shuttles.

❏ Materials. Thick warp: 22/2 cottolin (50% cotton, 50% linen, 3000 yds/lb), in red, yellow, light aqua, pink, dark aqua, and rust, about 4 oz total. Thin warp: 16/2 unmercerized cotton (6720 yds/lb), brown, 2 oz. Thick weft: 1 thread 22/2 cottolin, brown, and 1 thread 8/2 unmercerized cotton (3600 yds/lb), black, wound together on bobbin, ½ lb each. Thin weft: 8/2 unmercerized cotton, rust, 4 oz. Rust sewing thread.

❏ Wind a warp of 188 ends cottolin following color order in *6*, 4 yds long for 4 placemats. Wind a separate warp of 188 ends 16/2 brown cotton 4 yds long.

❏ Sley one 8/2 and one 16/2 end in each dent of 12-dent reed, 24 epi; center for 15⅝".

❏ Thread following draft in *5*, (16/2 on odd shafts, 8/2 on even shafts); add one 8/2 end to each side for floating selvedges.

❏ Weave 1½" plain weave with rust cotton. Treadle *a–c* 4x; *a–b* 1x; weave another plain-weave hem. Insert a contrasting thread to mark cut line. Repeat for each mat. Beat so that motifs are somewhat elongated to compensate for take-up. Each mat should be about 23" long with relaxed tension (including hems) before finishing.

❏ Finish by securing raw edges with straight machine stitching. Machine wash, gentle, with regular detergent; air dry on padded clothesline; press with hot iron. Cut mats apart and overcast raw edges taking care not to stretch them. Turn up hems 2x and machine stitch carefully along a rust thread. ✄

6. Color order for placemats

(for thick warp threads read right to left with draft in 5)

23			red
10	10	10	yellow
14	14	14	lt aqua
10	10	10	pink
20		23	dk aqua
	20		rust

paired-tie thick 'n thin

Blesi Jan Blesi Jan Blesi Jan Blesi Jan Blesi Jan Blesi Jan Blesi Jan Blesi Jan Blesi Jan Blesi Jan Blesi **Jan Blesi** Jan Blesi Jan B

1a. Paired-tie draft

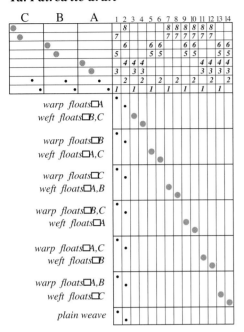

1b. Skeleton tie-up

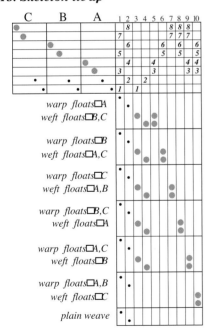

1c. Skeleton tie-up for a countermarch loom

> "I first encountered this weave structure several years ago in one of the **Handwoven Design Collections**. I referred to it for awhile as 'that random block structure that's sort of like summer and winter,' but that became a little cumbersome. I finally settled on calling it a 'paired-tie weave,' not because anyone else said it was, but because it seemed to fit. Anyway, I was more interested in making the structure work for me than in what to call it."

An examination of the threading units in *1a* shows their similarity to summer and winter units. Placing thick pattern threads in the warp as well as in the weft allows control of color changes in both warp and weft direction for remarkable design variation.

THE STRUCTURE

Paired-tie drafts do not share summer and winter's one-and-one threading and treadling of tie-down and pattern threads. Tie-down ends are paired in the threading, and tabby picks (which can be thought of as tie-down threads for warp floats) are paired in the treadling, thus the label: 'paired-tie' weave.

The threading

Each threading unit consists of four ends, a pair of fine tie-down ends followed by a pair of heavy pattern ends. The tie-down ends are threaded on shafts 1 and 2, and the pattern ends on the remaining shafts. Two pattern shafts are required for each block; eight shafts produce three blocks.

The treadling

Each treadling unit also consists of four threads: a pair of fine tabby threads followed by a pair of heavy pattern threads. On the pattern picks, pairs of warp ends are raised in the blocks where the pattern warp color is to show, and pairs of warp ends remain down where the pattern weft color is to show. The fine warp and weft threads form a plain-weave foundation throughout the entire piece. Threading a pair of tie-down ends at each selvedge gives a neat edge and precludes the need for a floating selvedge.

The tie-up

To weave pattern in all of the possible combinations of the four blocks would require many treadles. Two are required for tabby and two more for each block combination. The tie-up that produces warp floats in A, B, C, BC, AC, AB (weft floats in the other blocks) requires 14 treadles, as in *1a*. Two more treadles are required to weave warp floats in all three blocks and two more for weft floats in all three blocks.

A skeleton tie-up makes more block combinations possible with fewer treadles. One treadle is tied to raise shaft 1 and another to raise shaft 2. One pattern treadle is tied to raise each desired block combination. For the pattern picks, the treadle tied to raise shaft 1 is depressed with the selected pattern treadle and then the treadle tied to raise shaft 2 is depressed with the same pattern treadle; see *1b–c*.

Paired-tie advantages

The use of the heavy pattern threads in both warp and weft rather than in only the weft has many advantages. There are many options for controlling and enhancing color interaction. Interesting color effects can be achieved by changing threading and treadling blocks at different points from color changes in pattern warp and weft. The colors of the fine tie-down threads also influence the design: they can be dark or neutral and disappear into the background, or they can be bright and add spark. The colors of the pattern warp threads that are lowered peek through in the tie-down areas on the front and therefore influence the color mix in weft float areas.

Pattern threads with a bit of a sheen (pearl cotton, linnay, etc.) catch the light differently in the warp and weft directions to increase the contrast between pattern and background.

Because of the wide variety of ways that colors and textures can be mixed, designs woven in this structure appear more complex than they actually are.

Designing tips

Equally successful in this weave are designs in traditional block arrangements and designs with more contemporary random block arrangements. To design random block sizes and color orders in one of my pieces, I raided the game shelf and rounded up three dice. I assigned a weft yarn color to each face of the first die. I used the second die to determine the length of treadling blocks and the third to control the block combinations in the tie-up. I threw the dice about thirty times and wrote down the numbers each time. The outcome I called my 'Las Vegas runner'!

PAIRED-TIE THROW

- ❑ Equipment. 8-shaft loom, 40" weaving width; 15-dent reed; 2 shuttles with assorted bobbins for different-colored thick threads.
- ❑ Materials. Thin warp and weft: 20/2 wool (5600 yds/lb, Maine Line, JaggerSpun), Mushroom, 1/3 lb. Thick warp and weft: 18/2 wool/silk used doubled (5040 yds/lb, Zephyr, JaggerSpun) Cassis (C) 5 oz, Rosé (R) 4 oz, Teal (T) 1 oz, Mushroom (M) 2 oz. These amounts are sufficient for one throw, finished size 37" x 60" with 8" for sampling and 8" on both ends of throw for a plied fringe.
- ❑ Wind a warp of 392 doubled ends wool/silk and 394 single ends 20/2 Maine Line Mushroom 3 yds long in the color order shown in 2b.
- ❑ Sley 2-1-1-2-1-1 in a 15-dent reed. (Sley each pair of tie-down ends together in a dent; sley each strand of the doubled pattern end singly); there are 20 working ends per inch; center for 39¼".
- ❑ Thread following the draft in 3.
- ❑ Beam the warp under firm tension.
- ❑ Weave following the treadling sequence in 3 and the color order in 2a after 8" sampling to establish an even beat. (The skeleton tie-up is included in the draft in 3, not because it saves many treadles with this design, but to allow the addition of other pattern treadles for playing with other block combinations.)
- ❑ Finish by removing from loom. To secure the ends, prepare plied fringe by twisting two groups of eight warp threads separately in one direction; then twist them together in the opposite direction. Tie the ends in an overhand knot. Handwash in warm water with Orvus Paste or other mild soap; lay flat to dry.
- ❑ Tips. For best results when using 'paired-tie' weaves, sley the two working pattern ends in separate dents as for this project. When sleying 4/dent, separate the pattern end pairs and sley PttP–PttP (P = pattern; t = tie-down). Pearl cotton (3/2 for thick and 20/2 for thin) produces a throw with a soft drape when sleyed P-P-tt-P-P-tt in a 14-dent reed. The same thick warp yarn (3/2) with 10/2 for the thin warp yarn sleyed in a 15-dent reed makes an elegant table runner. Linnay at this same sett is a good weight for mats and runners. For added crispness, use 29/1 linen for the fine weft. 5/2 and 20/2 pearl cotton sleyed PttP-PttP in an 8-dent reed produce a firm and durable fabric for pillows or upholstery.

3. Draft for throw

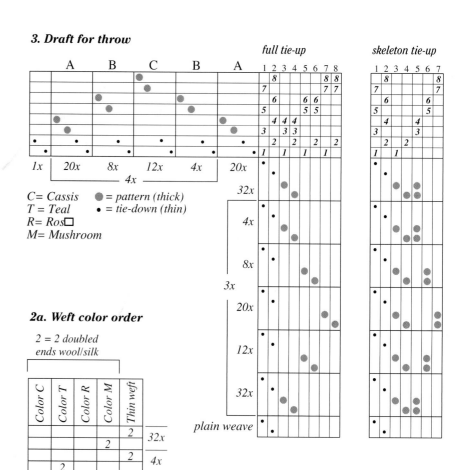

C = Cassis   ● = pattern (thick)
T = Teal   • = tie-down (thin)
R = Ros☐
M = Mushroom

full tie-up   *skeleton tie-up*

plain weave

2a. Weft color order

2 = 2 doubled ends wool/silk

Color C	Color T	Color R	Color M	Thin weft	
				2	32x
			2		
				2	4x
		2			
				2	8x
2					
				2	20x
			2		
				2	12x
2					
				2	32x
			2		
				2	4x
	2				
				2	8x
		2			
				2	20x
2					
				2	12x
		2			
				2	32x
			2		
				2	4x
	2				
				2	8x
2					
				2	20x
		2			
				2	12x
2					
				2	32x
			2		
				2	

2b. Warp color order

Color C	2				2		2 = 2 doubled
Color T			2				ends wool/silk
Color R				2			
thin warp	2	2	2	2	2		
	20x	4x	20x	20x	1x		

4x

thin thick 'n thin thick 'n thin thick 'n thin thick 'n thin thick 'n thin thick 'n thin thick 'n thin thick 'n thin thick 'n thin thick 'n thin thick 'r
thin thick 'n thin thick 'n thin thick 'n thin thick 'n thin thick 'n thin thick 'n thin thick 'n thin thick 'n thin thick 'n thin thick 'n thin thick 'n
thick 'n thin thick 'n thin thick 'n thin thick 'n thin thick 'n thin thick 'n thin thick 'n thin thick 'n thin thick 'n thin thick 'n thin thick 'n thin thick
thick 'n thin thick 'n thin thick 'n thin thick 'n thin thick 'n thin thick 'n thin thick 'n thin thick 'n thin thick 'n thin thick 'n thin thick 'n thin t

Use Jan's unusual 2-tie threading to display either thick warp colors or thick weft colors in random blocks for a contemporary look. Color choices can be soft and subtle like these, or bold and bright.

design a wardrobe with crackle

Kim Marie Bunke Kim Marie Bunke Kim Marie Bunke Kim Marie Bunke Kim Marie Bunke Kim Marie Bunke Kim Marie B

Cutting garment pieces on the bias is one way of getting diagonals, but bias fabric is not suitable for all garment shapes. Straight twills also produce diagonals, but they generate their own kind of drape.

Parallel shadow weave can be applied to a crackle threading system (see Parallel Shadow Weave, by Elizabeth Lang and Erica Dakin Voolich, Weavers Guild of Boston, 1987) to provide diagonal striping while the structure maintains a plain-weave base.

Let your experiments with shadow weave and crackle yield several garments instead of a box of samples tucked away in a closet. Try mixing thick and thin threads and dark and light threads to learn about color interaction, weave structure, sett, and effective placement of designs in garments.

1. Threading for parallel shadow weave based on crackle

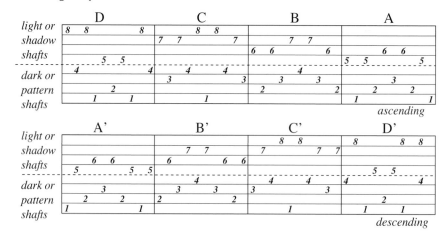

ascending

descending

2. Some orders of warp/weft colors and thicknesses

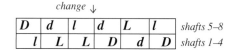

D = thick dark **L** = thick light **d** = thin dark **l** = thin light

Shadow weave uses alternating dark and light yarns in warp and weft to produce surface patterning known as color-and-weave effects. In the traditional shadow-weave threading system, each dark thread is followed by a light thread on the opposite shaft. Dark is usually considered pattern, and light, the 'shadow.' In 4-shaft shadow weave, 1(D) is opposed by 3(L), 2(D) by 4(L), 3(D) by 1(L), and 4(D) by 2(L). This system of opposites works well for designs based on simple twill lines. Drafting becomes confusing, however, with more complex twills or when shadow weave principles are applied to weave structures other than twill. Structural glitches often result; adjacent threads can fall on the same shaft, for example.

In a parallel shadow weave draft four additional shafts are used. Shaft 1(D) is opposed by 5(L), 2(D) by 6(L), 3(D) by 7(L), and 4(D) by 8(L). All the pattern (dark) ends are on one set of shafts and all the shadow ends (light) on another set for easier threading and a true tabby.

The crackle connection

Parallel shadow weave can be applied to a 4-shaft crackle threading system by inserting the shadow ends on shafts 5–8 between the ends of the crackle threading on shafts 1–4.

However, a crackle threading is actually a series of advancing 3-end point twills. When the necessary shadow-weave turning point rules are applied (dropping a thread at reversals) the resulting 'shadow' line is flattened and not exactly parallel; see the threading for shafts 5–8 in *1*.

When woven as crackle, the structure is no longer true shadow weave. Instead of alternating two wefts of the same size, pattern and shadow, in crackle a pattern (thick) weft alternates with a tabby (thin) weft.

Add thick and thin to the warp

Shadow weave depends on the color-and-weave effect of dark versus light for its surface patterning. Alternating thick and thin yarns yields another type of color-and-weave effect. The warping order in *2* shows some possibilities for alternating thick and thin threads *and* dark and light threads. Changing the thick/thin, dark/light order in either warp, weft, or both adds great variety to the potential designs.

From twills to block weaves

Like crackle, parallel shadow weave/crackle drafts can be considered block weaves and used with profile drafts. Several 4-block profile drafts are shown in *3a-e* p. 76. Blocks are threaded and woven in straight order to produce a diagonal design in the fabric in *Photo a*. The fabric in *Photo b* is produced from the profile draft in *3e*. The blocks in this draft are also arranged along a diagonal, but they vary in size.

Designing with diagonals

Placing diagonal stripes on garment fabric should be done with careful planning. For a top-and-bottom combination such as a dress or suit, I've found that arranging the diagonals as an 'X' across the body is best. It follows the natural shape and flatters the female form; see the suit fabric, p. 75.

Test before cutting the fabric by making an outline drawing of the garment shapes (simply trace the drawings on the front of the pattern envelope). Make lots of photocopies of the drawings and sketch different diagonal stripe placements on them. For a suit jacket, cut out a miniature paper jacket to double-check how the diagonals fold over on the collar and sleeves.

Once you've placed the diagonals, measure the pattern pieces and work out an efficient layout on graph paper. Since my loom is wide enough, I reverse the direction of the threading in the center, allowing pieces that are to be matched to be woven side by side. For a narrow warp the twill direction can be changed in the treadling.

Few diagonal designs are available in commercial fabric, possibly because one needs the reverse diagonal as well to make a symmetrical garment. (Note that flipping the fabric end for end does not reverse the direction of the diagonal.) Changing the direction of the diagonal in garment construction is something that handweavers can do much more easily than commercial manufacturers.

thin thick 'n thin th

Kim Marie Bunke Kim Marie Bunke Kim Marie Bunke Kim Marie Bunke Kim Marie Bunke Kim Marie B

Yarns in the blouse are all the same size (20/2 pearl cotton at 30 epi). In the Herb Gardening vest and hat, wide blocks are threaded in straight order, but treadled in broken order.

For the blouse and suit fabrics, blocks are threaded and woven in straight order. In the suit, both warp and weft alternate thick 'n thin threads (20/2 pearl cotton and 5/2 pearl cotton at 24 epi).

ck 'n thin thick 'n thin thick 'n thin thick 'n thin thick 'n thin thick 'n thin thick 'n thin thick 'n thin thick 'n thin
thin thick 'n thin thick 'n thin thick 'n thin thick 'n thin thick & thin thick 'n thin thick 'n thin thick 'n thin thick 'n
k 'n thin thick 'n thin thick 'n thin thick 'n thin thick 'n thin thick 'n thin thick 'n thin thick 'n thin thick 'n thin

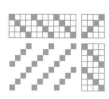

3a. 3-block profile, straight diagonals

3b. 4-block profile, broken diagonals

3c. 4-block profile, meandering diagonals

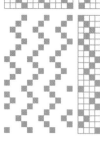

a. fabric woven from profile 3a.

Use threading units in 1 with treadling units in 4 to weave designs 3a–e.

4. Treadling units for fabrics in Photos a and b

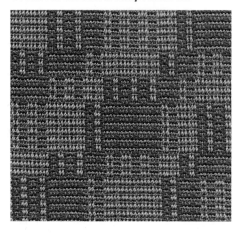

b. fabric woven from profile 3e.

3e. 4-block profile, diagonal blocks in varying sizes

3d. 4-block profile, varying block size

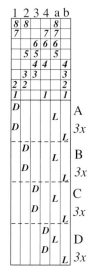

HERB GARDENING HAT

- ❏ Equipment. 8-shaft loom, 24" weaving width; 18-dent (or 12-dent) reed; 2 shuttles.
- ❏ Materials. Warp: 20/2 pearl cotton (8400 yds/lb), violet, 718 yds (1½ oz); 10/2 cotton (4200 yds/lb), dusty pink, 718 yds (3 oz). Weft: 20/2 cotton, deep lilac, 476 yds (1 oz); 10/2 cotton, deep lilac, 476 yds (2 oz). McCall's pattern P300 or 6077 (or similar baseball hat pattern).
- ❏ Wind a warp of 864 ends, 1⅜ yds long, alternating one strand 20/2 cotton and one strand 10/2 cotton. Add doubled 10/2 floating selvedges if desired. Note that in the warp, a thin end is followed by a thick end.
- ❏ Sley 2/dent in an 18-dent reed (or 3/dent in 12-dent reed: 2 ground ends with 1 pattern end, 2 pattern with 1 ground end); center for 24".
- ❏ Thread following the draft in *5*.

5. Draft for Herb Gardening hat

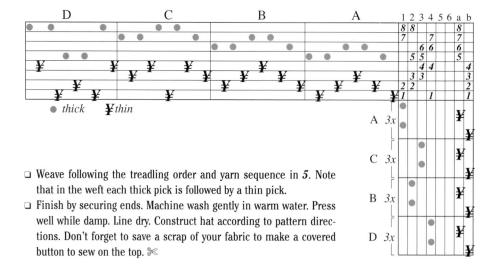

- ❏ Weave following the treadling order and yarn sequence in *5*. Note that in the weft each thick pick is followed by a thin pick.
- ❏ Finish by securing ends. Machine wash gently in warm water. Press well while damp. Line dry. Construct hat according to pattern directions. Don't forget to save a scrap of your fabric to make a covered button to sew on the top. ✄

thin thick 'n thin thick 'n thin thick 'n thin thick 'n thin thick 'n thin thick 'n thin thick 'n thin thick 'n thin thick 'n thin thick 'n
thin thick 'n thin thick 'n thin thick 'n thin thick 'n thin thick 'n thin thick 'n thin thick 'n thin thick 'n thin thick 'n thin thick 'n
thick 'n thin thick 'n thin thick 'n thin thick 'n thin thick 'n thin thick 'n thin thick 'n thin thick 'n thin thick 'n thin thick
thick 'n thin thick 'n thin thick 'n thin thick 'n thin thick 'n thin thick 'n thin thick 'n thin thick 'n thin thick 'n thin t

one, two, three vest

unke *Kim Marie Bunke* *Kim Marie Bunke* *Kim Marie Bunke* **Kim Marie Bunke** *Kim Marie Bunke* Kim M

Three coordinating fabrics, two treadling orders, and one threading and one warp produce the versatile, tailored vest on p. 78. The structure is a happy marriage of shadow weave and crackle that invites a weaver to mix colors in warp stripes. A color-and-weave pinstripe effect is the surprising result. Warp colors are analogous on the color wheel, and thick and thin threads alternate in both warp and weft.

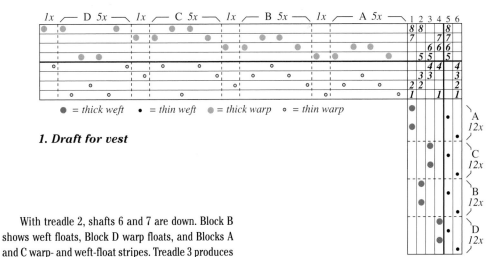

● = *thick weft*   • = *thin weft*   ● = *thick warp*   ○ = *thin warp*

1. Draft for vest

The vest is one of a series of garments woven in this unusual structure (see other examples on p. 75). The three different fabrics produced on the same threading coordinate perfectly with the pieced sections of the vest.

THICK 'N THIN CRACKLE

In this system, thick and thin threads in contrasting colors alternate in the warp. The thick and thin weft threads can be the same or other contrasting colors for a variety of effects.

The threading

The threading for this adaptation of shadow weave and crackle produces four blocks on eight shafts; see the draft in *1*. Thin ends (20/2 pearl cotton for this vest) are threaded on shafts 1–4 and thick ends (10/2 pearl cotton for this vest) are threaded on shafts 5–8. The color of the thick threads changes after each 168-thread repeat of the threading draft.

The tie-up

Notice in the tie-up that treadles 5 and 6 are used to insert the thin weft, which weaves tabby with thick and thin warp threads together. Treadles 1–4, the 'pattern' treadles, raise the thick threads in pairs to form the pattern blocks.

The treadling

Examine treadle 1 and the treadling sequence for Block A. The thick warp threads on shafts 5 and 6 are down for the two thick picks, so the thick weft shows in Block A where it passes over 6-3-6. In Block C, shafts 7 and 8 remain up for three picks; Block C shows 3-thread warp floats. Since shaft 7 is up in Block B (and 6 is down) and shaft 8 is up in Block D (and 5 is down), narrow stripes of warp floats and weft floats appear in these two blocks.

With treadle 2, shafts 6 and 7 are down. Block B shows weft floats, Block D warp floats, and Blocks A and C warp- and weft-float stripes. Treadle 3 produces weft floats in C, warp floats in A, and stripes in B and C. Treadle 4 produces weft floats in D, warp floats in B, and stripes in A and C.

Color-and-weave effects

The description of the interlacement does not cover the effects produced by color. The analogous colors used in the warp for the vest range from blue green to red violet. The weft color choice is very important. A color much darker than the warp enhances the color-and-weave effects.

Amazingly different pinstripe designs occur in each block. There are distinct dark, medium-dark, medium-light, and light blocks. They contribute to an appearance of movement and gradation across the fabric. The warp colors seem to blend although they are actually very distinct stripes. Such simple means can yield very interesting fabrics!

Advantages for clothing

Although this weave produces floats, the floats are limited to three threads (as in summer and winter and crackle), and the fabric has a stable plain-weave base. The cloth can therefore be cut in any direction, an ideal characteristic for garment fabric. If the difference in size between the thick and thin threads is not very great, the fabric also has a supple hand.

Repeating the treadling of any single block for some length produces narrow vertical stripes. The fabric can be turned in garments so that the stripes are horizontal, which provides the second fabric design in the vest. Weaving each block to square in broken-twill order (A, C, B, then D) creates the checkerboard pattern used for the third fabric design in the vest.

THE VEST

❑ Equipment. 8-shaft loom, 33" weaving width; 18- or 12-dent reed; 2 shuttles.

❑ Materials. Thick warp: 10/2 pearl cotton (4200 yds/lb), medium blue green, 630 yds (2½ oz); medium red violet, 420 yds (2 oz); medium blue, 420 yds (2 oz). Thin warp: 20/2 pearl cotton (8400 yds/lb), light blue green, 1470 yards (3 oz). Thick weft: 10/2 pearl cotton, dark red violet, 940 yds (4 oz); Thin weft: 20/2 pearl cotton, dark red violet, 940 yds (2 oz). Simplicity pattern 9058, buttons and other sewing notions required by pattern.

❑ Wind a warp of 1176 total ends (588 ends 20/2, 588 ends 10/2), 2½ yds long, holding together one strand 20/2 cotton and one strand 10/2 cotton in the following color order for 10/2, 84x each: medium blue green, medium red violet, medium blue, medium blue green, medium red violet, medium blue, medium blue green. Add doubled 10/2 ends to each side for floating selvedges if desired.

❑ Sley 2/dent in an 18-dent reed (or 3/dent in a 12-dent reed), 36 epi, center for 32²/₃".

❑ Thread following the draft in *1*, 7x.

❑ Weave following the treadling in *1*. Note that a thick pick is always followed by a thin pick. Weave the stripe section by repeating Block A. Weave the checkerboard by repeating the sequence for each block 12x. Weave 36" of stripes and 12" of checks.

❑ Finish by securing ends. Machine wash gently in warm water. Press well while still damp. Line dry. Construct vest according to pattern directions, cutting fronts and back on straight grain of stripe section, sides on cross grain, and bottom band on the checkerboard section of the fabric. ✄

thick 'n thin thick 'n thin

kissin' cousins of thick 'n thin

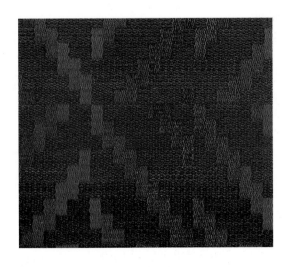

thick 'n thin throw

Deborah Harrison Deborah Harrison Deborah Harrison Deborah Harrison **Deborah Harrison** Deborah

1. 8-shaft draft for throw

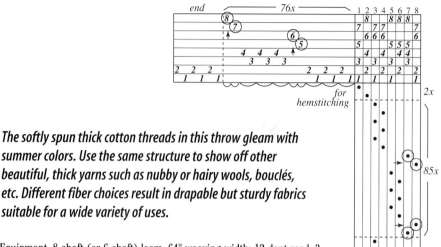

2. 6-shaft draft for throw

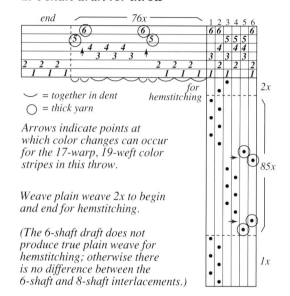

⌣ = together in dent

○ = thick yarn

Arrows indicate points at which color changes can occur for the 17-warp, 19-weft color stripes in this throw.

Weave plain weave 2x to begin and end for hemstitching.

(The 6-shaft draft does not produce true plain weave for hemstitching; otherwise there is no difference between the 6-shaft and 8-shaft interlacements.)

The softly spun thick cotton threads in this throw gleam with summer colors. Use the same structure to show off other beautiful, thick yarns such as nubby or hairy wools, bouclés, etc. Different fiber choices result in drapable but sturdy fabrics suitable for a wide variety of uses.

- ❑ Equipment. 8-shaft (or 6-shaft) loom, 64" weaving width; 12-dent reed; 3 shuttles; temple or stretcher bar (optional but very helpful for preventing crowding/breaking of selvedge threads).
- ❑ Materials. Thin warp and weft: 10/2 pearl cotton (4200 yds/lb, Silk City, Halcyon) in several compatible colors, 1½ oz for each of 17 stripes. Thick warp and weft: Cotton Classic (987 yds/lb, Tahki Yarns), Rowan Cotton Glacé, and/or Reynolds Gypsy (or other sportweight cotton 800–1000 yd/lb) in colors relating to thin ends, 2 oz for each of 17 stripes.
- ❑ Wind a warp 3½ yds long of 918 thin ends and 306 thick ends in 17 color stripes; see color chart for colors used here. Each of the 17 stripes consists of 9 'blocks' (6 thin ends with 1 thick before, 1 thick after), 54 thin and 18 thick ends each stripe. Changes from one color stripe to another occur between the two thick ends in a pair (see arrows in *1* and *2*).
- ❑ Sley thin ends 2/dent and thick ends 1/dent (19.2 epi) as indicated in the drafts in *1* and *2* (except drop the first and last thick end and sley the 12 thin ends that remain at either selvedge 3/dent); center for 63¼".
- ❑ Thread following *1* or *2*.
- ❑ Weave following *1* or *2* at 19.2 ppi. Allow 12" for fringe at both ends. The thick ends enclose the adjacent thin ends within a grid. To maintain grid squares at the selvedges, the thick weft must be locked into place with each shuttle change. For this purpose observe the following shuttle order: Shuttle 1, thin weft, 6 picks, beginning and ending on the right; Shuttle 2, thick weft A, 1 pick from right; Shuttle 3, thick weft B, 1 pick from left; Shuttle 1 repeat as above; Shuttle 3, thick weft B, 1 pick from right; Shuttle 2 thick weft A, 1 pick from left. When changing shuttles, pass the new shuttle under the previous weft thread if the selvedge block is down. If the selvedge block is up, pass the new shuttle over the previous weft thread. Arrange number of threads and colors in weft stripes exactly as warp stripes, adding two weft stripes, for a total of 19. Advance temple often.
- ❑ Finish by hemstitching (optional; work hemstitching over 4 picks tabby and 3 thin or 2 thick ends). Prepare twisted fringe: each fringe includes two bouts: 2 thick ends as one bout and the 3 thin ends on both sides of the thick pair as the other (at selvedges twist 2 thick ends and 3 groups thin). Machine wash, warm water, gentle cycle, mild detergent. Machine dry, low heat. Remove immediately. No ironing! Shrinkage is 7–8%.

Color considerations

Texture is emphasized if the thick threads are noticeably darker or lighter than the thin threads. Increase interest by using different but related hues and/or values for a few of the thin ends in each of the main colors, as illustrated in this throw. Changes in the colors of the thick threads need not always coincide with changes in the colors of the thins—there is limitless opportunity for color manipulation! ✄

COLOR CHART

U=UKI 10/2, S=Silk City 10/2, R=Rowan Cotton Glacé, T=Tahki Cotton Classic, G=Reynolds Gypsy

	Thick	Thin
1	U77 Dusty Coral	R783 (peach)
2	S132 Gold Brocade	R795 (yellow)
3	S300 Willow	G57 (dark teal)
4	U107 Melon	R738 (melon)
5	S42 Hemp	T3752 (light green)
6	U123 Phosphate	T3469 (mauve)
7	U134 Cactus	G71 (light turquoise)
8	Same as 2	Same as 2
9	Same as 5	Same as 5
10	Same as 4	Same as 4
11	U134 Cactus	T3774 (turquoise)
12	Same as 6	Same as 6
13	Same as 2	Same as 2
14	Same as 5	Same as 5
15	Same as 4	Same as 4
16	Same as 3	Same as 3
17	Same as 1	Same as 1

thin thick 'n thin t

on Deborah Harrison Deborah Harrison Deborah Harrison Deborah Harrison Deborah Harrison Deb

The draft for this throw is similar to the draft for diversified plain weave, except here thick threads form a frame around groups of thin threads, providing a unique opportunity for playing with color.

thick 'n thin thick 'n thin thick 'n thin thick 'n thin thick 'n thin thick 'n thin thick 'n thin thick 'n thin thick 'n thin thick 'n thin thick 'n thin thick
thin thick 'n thin thick 'n thin thick 'n thin thick 'n thin thick 'n thin thick 'n thin thick 'n thin thick 'n thin thick 'n thin thick 'n thin thick
ck 'n thin thick 'n thin thick 'n thin thick 'n thin thick 'n thin thick 'n thin thick 'n thin thick 'n thin thick 'n thin thick 'n thin thick 'n thin thick

pizza cloth for four, eight, or sixteen

Alice Schlein Alice Schlein Alice Schlein Alice Schlein Alice Schlein Alice Schlein **Alice Schlein** Alice Schlein Alice Sc

"Thick crust! Thin crust! Double crust! Pizza as you like it!" shouted the sign I drove past every day last spring. I was dieting, and all I could think about was pizza!

On my loom was a double weave fabric; the idea of thick-and-thin double weave began to claim my attention. Why not weave two layers of plain weave fabric simultaneously, I thought, one with a thick yarn in a coarse sett, and the other with a thin yarn in a finer sett?

'Pizza cloth,' or thick-and-thin double weave, can be executed on simple or complex looms; the versions here use four, eight, or 16 shafts. It is amenable to all sorts of yarns, as long as they are smooth and strong enough for normal double weave. It is easy to warp—both yarns are warped, chained, and beamed together, so only one warp beam is required.

SOME CONVENTIONS

Whether you are weaving pizza cloth on four, eight, or 16 shafts, these characteristics are common to all:

❑ The yarn for the thick layer is sett slightly more openly than it would be for single-layer plain weave (to provide the necessary 'breathing room' for the yarns of the two layers to slip past each other). The yarn for the thin layer is sett exactly twice as densely as the thick layer. For example, if the thick layer is sett at 10 epi, the thin layer is sett at 20 epi, for a total sett of 30 epi. The weft yarns are the same size as the warp yarns, and the picks per inch are the same as the ends per inch for balanced cloth on both layers.

❑ The warping order is *always* one thick end, two thin ends, repeat. The weft order is *always* one thick pick, two thin picks, repeat.

❑ The thick warp ends are threaded on the odd-numbered shafts, and the thin warp ends are threaded on the even-numbered shafts, no matter how many shafts are used.

Four-shaft version

To weave pizza cloth on four shafts, follow the draft in *1*. If you are using a loom with fewer than eight treadles, you will have to modify the tie-up and depress two treadles at the same time to achieve the correct sheds. Complete all six picks of a rotation before switching from one stripe to another. Horizontal stripes of any size can be woven; any

a. Pizza cloth on four shafts

b. Pizza cloth on eight shafts

1. Draft for 4-shaft pizza cloth

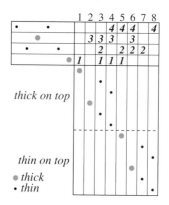

2. Draft for 8-shaft pizza cloth

individual stripe will have thick plain weave cloth on one side and thin on the reverse. A four-shaft sample in alpaca and rayon is shown in *Photo a*.

Eight-shaft version

Use the threading and treadling units in *2* to weave pizza cloth on eight shafts. A block that weaves thick

on the face of the cloth weaves thin on the reverse, and vice versa. Any 2-block profile can be chosen for translation to eight-shaft pizza cloth. Every square in the profile threading draft is replaced by a 6-end threading unit and every square in the profile treadling draft is replaced by a 6-pick treadling unit. *Photo b* shows an 8-shaft sample in alpaca and rayon.

thin thick 'n thin thick 'n thin thick 'n thin thick 'n thin thick 'n thin thick 'n thin thick 'n thin thick 'n thin thick 'n thin
thin thick 'n thin thick 'n thin thick 'n thin thick 'n thin thick 'n thin thick 'n thin thick 'n thin thick 'n thin thick 'n thin thick 'n
'n thin thick 'n thin thick 'n thin thick 'n thin thick 'n thin thick 'n thin thick 'n thin thick 'n thin thick 'n thin thick 'n thin
thick 'n thin thick 'n thin thick 'n thin thick 'n thin thick 'n thin thick 'n thin thick 'n thin thick 'n thin thick 'n thin thick 'n thin t

Fast food? Fancy food? Fabulous table settings to feast the eyes!

3a. Threading units for 16-shaft pizza cloth

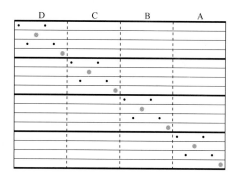

3b. Tie-up and treadling units for 16-shaft pizza cloth

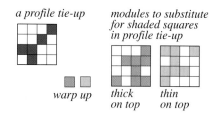

a profile tie-up

modules to substitute for shaded squares in profile tie-up

warp up

thick on top

thin on top

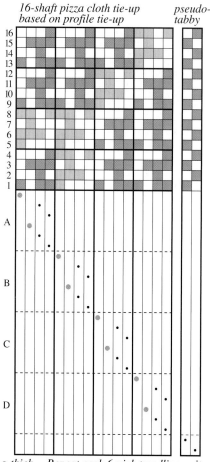

16-shaft pizza cloth tie-up based on profile tie-up

pseudo-tabby

● thick   Repeat each 6-pick treadling unit
· thin   for the desired length of the block

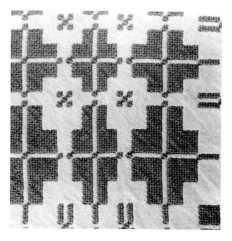

c. 16-shaft pizza cloth: four blocks

d. Networked pizza cloth

e. Networked pizza cloth

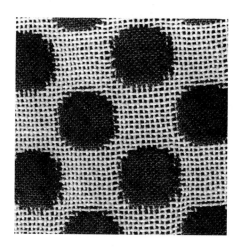

f. Networked pizza cloth

Two sixteen-shaft versions —decisions, decisions!

Sixteen-shaft pizza cloth is a gourmet weaver's delight. If you have a conventional 16-shaft treadle loom, you can draft pizza cloth from any four-block profile (four shafts are required for each block as with regular double weave). The threading units are shown in *3a* and the tie-up and treadling information in *3b* for the four possible blocks. For further details, see **Photo c** and the project notes for the Angstadt pizza cloth placemats, p. 87.

If you have a 16-shaft loom with a dobby head, either mechanical or computer-assisted, you can enjoy networked pizza cloth and break away from block constraints. The particular draft I have devised to illustrate networked pizza is a pattern of staggered circles on a plain ground. When one layer of the cloth shrinks more than the other, the appearance of the fabric is like—you guessed it!—my favorite pizza, so I have named the draft for this cloth Pepperoni. See *4–6* and **Photo d**.

For those of you who would like to design your own networked pizza cloth, see *4* for the initial and the network for developing a threading draft from a pattern line. The dobby pegging templates for the thick layer and the thin layer are shown in *6a*; these are expanded and then cut and pasted following a selected pattern line. (For a refresher course on network drafting, refer to *Weaver's*, Issues 6, 7, 8, and 10, and *Network Drafting: An Introduction,* by Alice Schlein, 1994.)

As with all other versions of pizza cloth, networked pizza (including Pepperoni) is threaded one thick end, two thin ends, repeat; and woven one thick pick, two thin picks, repeat.

NETWORK DRAFTING PRIMER

Here is a review of network drafting terms and procedures. You can weave Pepperoni without understanding network drafting simply by following the threading and treadling plans.

thin thick 'n thin thick 'n thin thick 'n thin thick 'n thin thick 'n thin thick 'n thin thick 'n thin thick 'n thin thick 'n thin thick 'n
thin thick 'n thin thick 'n thin thick 'n thin thick 'n thin thick 'n thin thick 'n thin thick 'n thin thick 'n thin thick 'n thin thick 'n
thin thick 'n thin thick 'n thin thick 'n thin thick 'n thin thick 'n thin thick 'n thin thick 'n thin thick 'n thin thick 'n thin thick
thin 'n thin thick 'n thin thick 'n thin thick 'n thin thick 'n thin thick 'n thin thick 'n thin thick 'n thin thick 'n thin thick 'n thin t

Network drafting terms:

- *initial*: a threading group, much like a threading unit but more freely formed, that is used to build a threading grid (network) of more than one initial.
- *network*: A base grid containing initials repeated horizontally and vertically on which the actual threading is plotted.
- *digitizing*: reducing a threading profile to one that uses fewer horizontal rows (hence fewer shafts) by substituting one shaft for two (or more).
- *telescoping*: reducing a threading profile to one that uses fewer horizontal rows (hence fewer shafts) by returning to the first row of the draft to thread segments that extend beyond the shafts available.
- *pattern line*: a continuous line drawn on a threading grid that becomes the basis for a pattern drawdown.
- *harmonics*: parallel or incidental curves appearing in a pattern drawdown when a pattern line has been reduced by telescoping.

Steps for network drafting

- Draw a pattern line on graph paper.
- Reduce the pattern line by digitizing or telescoping.
- Place the pattern line on a network (as in *4*) made of repeats of the initial.
- Generate the actual threading by first filling the 'hits.' Then fill in the next marked network square above the pattern line in each of the columns where there are misses.
- Prepare templates in units of basic weaves for the number of shafts threaded (as in *6a* but extended to as many horizontal rows as the number of picks intended).
- Plot a pattern line for the treadling and trace the pattern line on one of the templates.
- Cut out the traced piece(s) and overlay them in on the other template.

Note the two half-circles of thick-on-top placed on the template of thin-on-top (*6b*).

4. Initial and network for pizza cloth threading

6a. Templates for cut-and-paste pizza cloth peg plan

thick on top

thin on top

6b. Pepperoni peg plan

5. Threading for Pepperoni

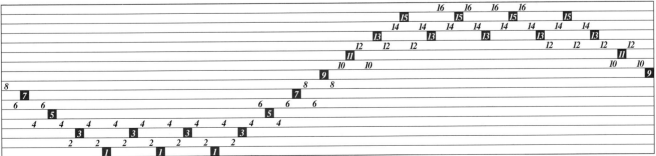

Suitable yarns and uses

Some yarn combinations which work well for all versions of pizza cloth are:

❑ Heavy cotton flake at 8 epi with 5/2 pearl cotton at 16 epi, total sett 24 epi, for casual heavy jacket material (shown in *Photo d*).

❑ 4/4 cotton at 8 epi with 10/2 pearl cotton at 16 epi, total sett 24 epi, for heavy placemats (shown in *Photo c*).

❑ 5/2 pearl cotton at 10 epi with 10/2 rayon at 20 epi, total sett 30 epi, for a sporty medium-weight blouse or jacket fabric.

❑ 12/2 cotton at 12 epi and 20/2 pearl cotton at 24 epi, total sett 36 epi, for lightweight tailored vest fabric (shown in *Photo d*).

❑ My personal favorite: 3-ply alpaca, 1830 yds/lb, from Henry's Attic, at 10 epi; and 10/2 rayon, from Scott's Woolen Mill, Inc., at 20 epi; total sett 30 epi, for a very special bubbly fabric (shown in *Photos a, b,* and *d*). The alpaca and rayon wind together beautifully in one warp and produce no tension problems whatever. When the woven fabric is washed, the rayon shrinks 12% but the alpaca doesn't shrink at all, giving a pronounced 3-D effect to the finished cloth.

Many other yarn sizes, combinations, and setts are possible. Experiment by sampling to find the ones appropriate for specific fabric uses.

Preparing to weave

Warps for all versions of pizza cloth can easily be wound by holding three warp ends (one thick and two thin) together as one in the winding of the warp and the forming of the crosses. When threading the heddles, simply pick up the appropriate warp end (thick or thin according to the draft) from the group of three. If you lightly separate the three warp ends

7. Angstadt pizza placemat profile draft

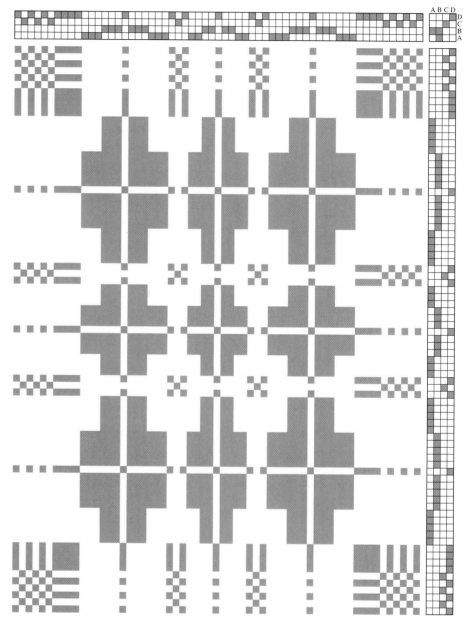

with the fingers of one hand as you wind the warp (behaving as a human warping paddle), the possibility of tangles is minimized. It is not necessary to use two warp beams for the two different fibers.

Various denting arrangements can be employed for pizza cloth. The most convenient is three per dent (one thick and two thin); consequently, an 8-dent reed works well for a 24 epi warp, 10-dent reed for 30 epi, and 12-dent reed for 36 epi. If you warp from front to back (sley the reed, thread the heddles, and then wind warp on beam), three ends per dent is

the only arrangement you can use. But if you warp from back to front (spread in a raddle, beam, thread the heddles, and then sley the reed) other denting schemes are also practical. For instance, with a 12-dent reed, warping back to front, you can sley 1 thick end and 1 thin end in the first dent, 1 thin and 1 thick in the second, 2 thin in the third, and repeat, for an effective sett of 8 epi thick layer and 16 epi thin layer. Any reed marks in these cloths will disappear in the first washing. Just be sure that the thicker yarn can pass easily through the chosen reed.

thick 'n thin thin thick 'n thin thick 'n thin thick 'n thin thick 'n thin thick 'n thin thick 'n thin thick 'n thin t

With a 16-shaft loom, weave pizza cloth in any 4-block design. Substitute the threading units from **3a** for each square of the profile threading draft. Substitute the thin-on-top and thick-on-top modules in **3b** for corresponding filled-in and blank squares of a profile tie-up. Placemats are especially appropriate woven in thick/thin double weave—the two-layer fabric is firm, flat, and durable. Garments that require a sturdy cloth such as vests and outerwear are also lovely in this fabric, especially since 'pizza cloth' provides such great potential for playing with color.

ANGSTADT PIZZA PLACEMATS

A section of profile draft no. 36 from *Jacob Angstadt Designs Drawn from His Weavers Patron Book** is adjusted slightly and adapted so that its proportions suit a placemat format; the resulting profile is translated into pizza cloth.

- ❑ Equipment. 16-shaft loom, 16" weaving width; 8-dent reed; 2 shuttles.
- ❑ Materials. 4/4 cotton (840 yds/lb, Mo-Purl Yarns, Inc., 318 E. Samford Ave., Auburn, AL 36830), hot pink, 2 lbs; 10/2 pearl cotton (4200 yds/lb, Halcyon), yellow and turquoise, ½ lb each. These estimates are generous. If buying the 10/2 pearl on 300-yd cones, buy 5 cones each of yellow and turquoise. (It is always a good idea if making substitutions to check all yarns for colorfastness.)
- ❑ Wind a warp of 366 ends, 6 yds long, as follows: 1 end hot pink, 2 ends turquoise, 20x; 1 end hot pink, 2 ends yellow, 12x; 1 end hot pink, 2 ends turquoise, 2x; 1 end hot pink, 2 ends yellow, 12x; 1 end hot pink, 2 ends turquoise, 6x; 1 end hot pink, 2 ends yellow, 8x; 1 end hot pink, 2 ends turquoise, 2x; 1 end hot pink, 2 ends yellow, 8x; 1 end hot pink, 2 ends turquoise, 6x; 1 end hot pink, 2 ends yellow, 12x; 1 end hot pink, 2 ends turquoise, 2x; 1 end hot pink, 2 ends yellow, 12x; 1 end hot pink, 2 ends turquoise, 20x.

A 6-yd warp provides six placemats with hems, a generous amount of loom waste, and 15% take-up and shrinkage. When winding the warp, hold one thick and two thin ends together as one, lightly separating them with the fingers. Treat the three ends as one in forming the threading cross.

- ❑ Spread the warp in a raddle, centered for 15¼", and wind on a single warp beam.

- ❑ Thread the thick-and-thin warp following the profile draft in **7**. For every block in the threading profile, substitute six ends of the appropriate thread-by-thread draft in **3a**, picking up a thick or thin warp end as needed. For example, since the first unit in the threading draft profile in **7** is in Block D, the first six warp ends are threaded: thick end on shaft 13, thin on 14, thin on 16, thick on 15, thin on 14, thin on 16.
- ❑ Sley three ends (one thick and two thin) in each dent of an 8-dent reed for 24 epi; center for 15¼".
- ❑ Weave following the profile draft in **7**, substituting the appropriate 6-pick treadling unit from **3b** for each unit of the treadling profile. Weft order is one thick pick, two thin picks. The thick weft is hot pink 4/4 cotton throughout. The thin weft is turquoise in blocks C and D, and yellow in blocks A and B. Beat to achieve a balanced cloth, that is, eight ppi thick layer and 16 ppi thin layer. For the hems, alternately raise all thick ends and all thin ends for a pseudo-tabby, using one of the thin yarns as weft. Weave 1½" for each hem, and a shot of a contrasting yarn to separate mats.
- ❑ Finish by cutting the mats from the loom in one long piece. Zigzag the two ends to prevent ravelling, wash the piece by machine in warm water, mild detergent. Machine dry until barely damp, steam press vigorously, cut mats apart, turn ends under ½" twice and hem by hand. Get out your best silver and phone for pizza! ✂

*Holroyd, Ruth N., and Beck, Ulrike L., *Jacob Angstadt Designs Drawn from his Weavers Patron Book*, Ruth Holroyd, 1976.

color control through thick and thin

Doramay Keasbey *Doramay Keasbey* *Doramay Keasbey* **Doramay Keasbey** *Doramay Keasbey* *Doramay Keasbey Doramay*

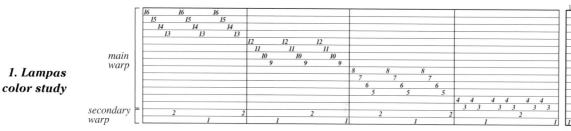

**1. Lampas
color study**

main warp

secondary warp

Two very different weave structures provide solutions to two very different challenges for woven arrangements of the colors of the spectrum. What they have in common are the use of full-strength hues in the warp and the control of where and how the colors appear through the appropriate placement of thick or thin weft threads.

Color variation in lampas is generally provided by the secondary pattern (thick) weft. What if, instead, color variety is produced as a result of the capacity of the main weave to be several different structures?

COLOR IN LAMPAS

Lampas is a double weave that produces clearly defined blocks with a strong contrast in texture between pattern and background areas. The interaction of varied colors in the fine warp and weft of the main weave can be set off by solid-color frames formed by the thick pattern weft in the weft-faced secondary weave. In this color study (see the lower photo, p. 89), the secondary warp is threaded for plain weave on the first two shafts, leaving the remaining shafts available for the main warp. The more shafts that are available for the main warp, the more variety is possible in both structure and pattern.

Reduced to barest essentials, this color study can be woven on six shafts as a 2-block window-pane effect in which both the main and secondary structures are plain weave. Sixteen shafts threaded as in *1* provide three main-weave blocks—each of which can produce plain weave or twill—as well as a fourth plain-weave block. In *1*, shafts 1 and 2 are reserved for the secondary warp, shafts 3 and 4 for the dark plain-weave block that acts to separate the color blocks, and the remaining 12 shafts are used for the colored 'windows.'

Main weave: damask?

The stimulus for this color adventure is a seemingly innocent statement tucked away in the definition of 'lampas' in the 1964 English version of the CIETA vocabulary: "figured textiles in which a pattern, composed of weft floats bound by a binding warp, is added to a ground fabric formed by a main warp and a main weft. The ground may be tabby, twill, satin, damask, etc...."

Damask! Even a few blocks of damask—warp satin contrasting with weft satin—*without* a secondary structure require a fairly sophisticated loom. So the suggestion that the main structure may itself be a figured textile to be further decorated by pattern floats held in place by an additional secondary warp raises numerous questions. Where are examples of lampas that illustrate this? Where were they woven, by whom, when, and—most importantly—*how*? What kind of loom can provide pattern control for both the ground fabric *and* the secondary decorative elements? Without resorting to extremely tedious pick-up techniques, is such a complex structure feasible for today's handweavers?

Main weave: twill blocks

Suspecting that elaborate figuring in both the ground and the secondary structures might elude all but those who operate a Jacquard mechanism, I wondered if simplification of the structure might put this idea within the scope of a multishaft floor loom. In this lampas color study the dark separating frames are created by the secondary warp and a thick 'pattern' weft. Within each colored main weave window areas of 1/3, 2/2, and 3/1 twill are formed. (This is not really damask, but at least it suggests the principle of patterning within the main weave!) The twill blocks are combined in various ways within each window to emphasize at times the color of the warp, at others the weft, and sometimes a balanced mixture of both.

Twenty-one colors in the main warp are arranged to blend gradually in the order of a rainbow spectrum; three analogous hues appear side by side in each of the seven windows. The weft of the main fabric follows the same color order and proportions as the main warp. So far, these characteristics describe the format for a normal color blanket.

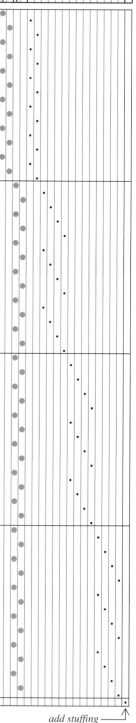

add stuffing ——

thin thick 'n thin thick 'n thin thick 'n thin thick 'n thin thick 'n thin thick 'n thin thick 'n thin thick 'n thin thick 'n thin thick 'n
thin thick 'n thin thick 'n thin thick 'n thin thick 'n thin thick 'n thin thick 'n thin thick 'n thin thick 'n thin thick 'n thin thick 'n
thick 'n thin thick 'n thin thick 'n thin thick 'n thin thick 'n thin thick 'n thin thick 'n thin thick 'n thin thick 'n thin thick
thin 'n thin thick 'n thin thick 'n thin thick 'n thin thick 'n thin thick 'n thin thick 'n thin thick 'n thin thick 'n thin thick
thick 'n thin thick 'n thin thick 'n thin thick 'n thin thick 'n thin thick 'n thin thick 'n thin thick 'n thin thick 'n thin th

Doramay Keasbey Doramay Keasbey Doramay Keasbey Doramay Keasbey Doramay Keasbey Doram.

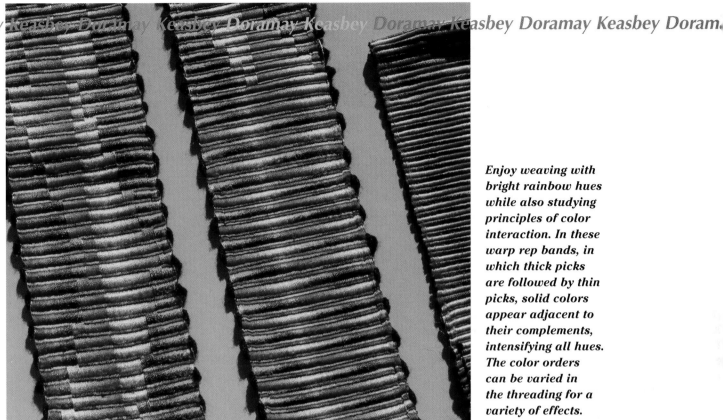

Enjoy weaving with bright rainbow hues while also studying principles of color interaction. In these warp rep bands, in which thick picks are followed by thin picks, solid colors appear adjacent to their complements, intensifying all hues. The color orders can be varied in the threading for a variety of effects.

Lampas allows different color mixes of fine warp and weft threads to be framed by a dark secondary weave, whose thick weft shows on the surface. In the mat, the thick secondary weft is a dark navy blue.

thick 'n thin thick 'n thin thick 'n thin thick 'n thin thick 'n thin thick 'n thin thick 'n thin thick 'n thin thick 'n thin thick 'n thin thick 'n thin thick 'n thin thick
thin thick 'n thin thick 'n thin thick 'n thin thick 'n thin thick 'n thin thick 'n thin thick & thin thick 'n thin thick 'n thin thick 'n thin thick 'n thin thick 'n thin thin
'n thin thick 'n thin thick 'n thin thick 'n thin thick 'n thin thick 'n thin thick 'n thin thick 'n thin thick 'n thin thick 'n thin thick 'n thin thick 'n thin thic

Secondary weave: window frames

The features that set this lampas version apart from the ordinary are the many possibilities for varying the color emphasis unexpectedly through the treadling of the main weave (showing more warp, more weft, or equal amounts of both) and, of course, the presence of the dark separating bands that showcase each colored square. The lampas structure enables these bands to be woven in such a way that the two fabrics are closely integrated wherever the dark weft floats on the surface.

Wherever the layers of lampas are not integrated the two layers are free, and pockets form between the ground and the underlying secondary fabric. Each colored square forms one of these pockets, which are stuffed with polyester fiber before being closed off by the integrating action of the succeeding dark bands. The outcome—lampas ravioli!

Color in warp rep

A second thick-and-thin color experiment investigates what happens when rainbow color spectrums interact. In this case two rainbow sequences are juxtaposed in such a way that each hue of one is countered in the other by its complement. The warp consists of two rainbows, one starting at one edge and ending at the other while the second begins at the center and, after reaching an edge, continues from the opposite edge back to the center.

Adjacent complements intensify hues

An interesting phenomenon of color perception is the seemingly heightened intensity of a hue when placed on a background of its complement. This is especially apparent when substantial amounts of each color are present so areas can be readily identified. In very small scale, such as with adjacent single threads, however, the visual mixing of complements may seem to dull the hues to a muddy neutral. To counteract this possibility, it helps to change the proportions so at least one color or set of related colors is large enough to be clearly discerned on its own.

In the warp rep example all color is in the warp, and selected colors show on the surface when raised to float over the weft. A thin weft creates an undistinguished fine line of raised warp, whereas a thick weft provides a much broader surface for the colored warp threads to float over. Patterns are produced by alternating the thick and thin wefts and selecting which warp colors float over which weft. The more shafts available, the greater the pattern selection can be.

RAINBOW RAYON REP BELT

As few as two shafts are enough to weave dazzling interlocking rainbows. Four shafts provide additional color control, and undulating twill patterns are possible with more than four. Try designing your own color rainbows, and study the juxtaposition of complementary colors at the same time! Belts make quick, easy, and ready-to-wear additions to any wardrobe. The fiber used for these belts is a lustrous rayon that heightens the impact of the rainbow colors.

❑ Equipment. 12-shaft loom (to sample all variations; sequences *2c* and *2e* require 12 shafts) or 4-shaft loom (for simplest effects, see treadling sequences *4a–4c*); 10-dent reed; 2 shuttles, one for thick weft and one for thin weft.

❑ Materials. Warp: fine rayon sewing thread (approximately 14,240 yds/lb or 890 yds/oz) in 12 hues; one 12-spool full-spectrum package of Natesh rayon from Aardvark Adventure (2880 total yds) provides four belts, each about 45" long. Thick weft: approximately 1 oz rayon ¼" ribbon, (Glacé, Stanley Berroco), black. Thin weft: approximately ½ oz rayon, silk, or cotton sewing thread, any color.

❑ Wind a warp of 384 ends 7½ yds long according to the color order in *3*: Arrange 12 colors in spectrum sequence, assigning a letter to each hue, for example, A = red; B = red orange; C = orange; D = orange yellow; E = yellow; F = yellow green; G = green; H = green blue; I = blue; J = blue violet; K = violet; L = violet red. Wind pairs of threads, representing opposites on the color wheel. These pairs are represented in *3* by each set of letters aligned vertically, i.e., wind two rainbows simultaneously. For smoothly graduated colors in each rainbow it is desirable to alternate old and new colors at each transition to a new color as indicated.

For example, to wind Block I: wind A and G once, L and F once, A and G once, L and F once, A and G eight times, B and H once, A and G once, B and H once, A and G once; then proceed to Block II. (Block I begins at one selvedge, and the colors blend into Block II, etc., continuing through Block VI at the center. The threading of Blocks I through VI repeats in the second half of the sequence, but notice that the color sequence is different in the second half (second column in *3*) in order to spread each of the two spectrums continuously across the entire width.

❑ Sley 20 ends per dent in 10-dent reed (200 epi); center for 1¹⁵⁄₁₆" width.

❑ Thread twelve shafts according to the draft in *2*, 32 ends per block. One of the rainbows begins

on shaft 1 in Block I and continues numerically through shaft 12 in the second Block VI. It is countered by the second rainbow beginning on shaft 7 in Block I and continuing through shaft 12 in Block VI followed by shaft 1 through shaft 6 in the second half. Following *3*, start threading with the warp color marked (*) in Block I. Thread each block 8x (32 ends). Thread the complete block sequence 2x, ending with the color at the asterisk in block VI at the opposite edge. For 4-shaft looms, using the same color orcer, alternate two blocks 24x each for 96 ends in each; see the draft in *4*.

❑ Weave the effect of your choice according to the treadling directions in *2* or *4* for 48" for each belt. Begin and end each belt with a few picks of plain weave to be turned under as a hem. (For plain weave hems, alternate treadles in sequence *2a* or *4a* using thin weft only.)

Sequences *2a* and *4a* produce the warp-faced ribs characteristic of warp rep alternating with the thin line produced by the thin weft. For variety in sequences *2a* and *4a*, reverse the order of thick and thin threads after each set of 11 picks (thick in pick 11 followed by thick in pick 12 to begin a new set of 11 picks), reversing the spectrum appearing on top for the thick pick. Sequences *2b* and *4b* introduce two thin picks between thick picks, alternating colors between the two spectrums. Sequences *2d* and *4c* form a checkerboard pattern by raising colors from alternate spectrums in alternate sections for a series of seven picks, then exchanging them for a series of seven. Sequence *2c* produces a diagonal pattern; sequence *2e* causes the diagonal to meander in a serpentine fashion.

During weaving, observe edge warp ends closely. Anchor any stray edge warp by wrapping the weft around it if the shed sequence allows an end to float.

❑ Finish after removing from the loom with two rows of straight machine stitching across the ends of each belt, catching the weft in the stitching of each row. Cut belts apart. Turn narrow hems at each end and sew invisibly by hand. ✂

2. 12-shaft draft for rainbow belt

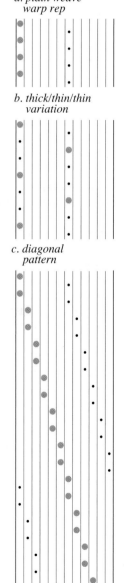
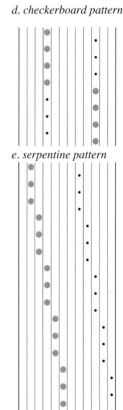

d. checkerboard pattern

a. plain weave warp rep

b. thick/thin/thin variation

e. serpentine pattern

c. diagonal pattern

3. Warp and weft color order for rainbow belts

Block I
*ALALAAAAAAAABABA
 GFGFGGGGGGGGHGHG

Block II
BABABBBBBBBBCBCB
HGHGHHHHHHHHIHIH

Block III
CECECCCCCCCCDCDC
IHIHIIIIIIIIJIJI

Block IV
DCDCDDDDDDDDEDED
JIJIJJJJJJJJKJKJ

Block V
EDEDEEEEEEEEFEFE
KJKJKKKKKKKKLKLK

Block VI
FEFEFFFFFFFFGFGF
LKLKLLLLLLLLALAL

Block I
GFGFGGGGGGGGHGHG
ALALAAAAAAAABABA

Block II
HGHGHHHHHHHHIHIH
BABABBBBBBBBCBCB

Block III
IHIHIIIIIIIIJIJI
CBCBCCCCCCCCDCDC

Block IV
JIJIJJJJJJJJKJKJ
DCDCDDDDDDDDEDED

Block V
KJKJKKKKKKKKLKLK
EDEDEEEEEEEEFEFE

Block VI
LKLKLLLLLLLLALAL
FEFEFFFFFFFFGFGF*

Example: threading for Block I (starting at *):
171717171717171717171717171717
AGLFAGLFAGAGAGAGAGAGAGAGBHAGBHAG

4. 4-shaft draft for rainbow belt

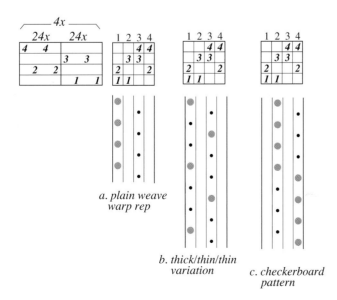

a. plain weave warp rep

b. thick/thin/thin variation

c. checkerboard pattern

ripped about rep

Rosalie Neilson Rosalie Neilson Rosalie Neilson Rosalie Neilson **Rosalie Neilson** Rosalie Neilson Rosali

Ripsmatta is the popular Swedish name for the weave structure also known as warp-faced rep or just warp rep. The name ripsmatta comes from the finished product, a rep-weave (rip) mat (matta). Whatever its name, it is fun to explore! Warp rep is a block weave in which two shafts are required for each block that produces pattern independently. Varying the color order in the threading results in elaborate patterns on even a limited number of shafts.

1a. Threading units for independent blocks on sixteen shafts

1b. Threading units for independent blocks on eight shafts

1c. Threading units for independent blocks on four shafts

1d. Four blocks weave 'two by two'

RIPSMATTA OR WARP-FACED REP

Warp rep is a technique in which the warp completely covers the weft. A very thick pick alternates with a a very thin pick in plain weave. If one color is used for all the warp threads, the effect is strictly textural—the surface is composed of horizontal ribs (i.e., the thick pick of weft) separated by narrow lines (the thin pick).

The simplest warp-faced rep structure is plain weave woven on two shafts. If all of the threads on shaft 1 are black and all of the threads on shaft 2 are white and shaft 1 is raised for the thick pick and shaft two for the thin pick, black horizontal ribs separated by thin white lines appear on the face of the cloth, and white horizontal ribs separated by thin black lines appear on the reverse.

Shafts 1 and 2 can be thought of as providing a block of color. If shaft 1 is raised for the thick pick, the block is black; if shaft 2 is raised for the thick pick, the block is white. Two-block designs, such as a checkerboard or a monk's belt motif, can be woven on two shafts if the color order in the threading is reversed from one block to the next. For example, if sections with black on 1, white on 2 alternate with sections of white on 1, black on 2, a checkerboard design occurs when shaft 1 is raised for the thick picks and 2 for the thin picks followed by shaft 2 raised for the thick picks and shaft 1 for the thin.

Two blocks can be woven on four shafts without altering the color order. If black is threaded on odd shafts and white on even (as in *1c*), either shaft can be raised for the thick pick and the other for the thin independently. The cloth can therefore show black in both blocks; white in both blocks; or black in one block, white in the other or vice versa.

Design techniques for rep

Since two shafts are required for each independent block of pattern, a 16-shaft loom provides eight

blocks. One shaft of each pair is threaded with a pattern color, and the other with a background color. Either color in each block can be selected to appear on the face for the thick pick.

My first 16-shaft, 8-block wall hanging was threaded in the most logical manner: the A block on shafts 1, 2; B on 3, 4; C on 5, 6; etc. Using 3/2 cotton at 30 epi, I spent hours threading the 54" wide warp. After I tied the warp to the front apron rod, I was aghast when I treadled my first shed—I could not get the warp threads to separate. Instead, the metal rod to which the warp was tied rose in an elliptical curve, matching the profile of my threading draft!

I now allow as much space as possible between the two ends of each block. The pattern ends are threaded on the first half of the shafts available and the background ends on the second half; see *1a–1c*. Even separating block threadings on four shafts so that A = 1, 3 and B = 2, 4 improves shed formation.

As a block weave, warp rep can be used with block profile drafts. The threading is a simple matter of substituting a designated number of P/B (pattern/background) pairs for squares in the selected profile threading draft (the exact number depends on the number of ends required for desired block width).

To translate the profile tie-up into an actual tie-up, think of the blocks marked in the profile tie-up as representing the corresponding pattern shafts to be raised for the thick pick. Therefore for 16 shafts, for example, an eight-block profile tie-up can be used exactly as is for the first eight pattern shafts on the first eight treadles. Since the background shafts 9–16 operate opposite to the pattern shafts, they are tied opposite to the first eight shafts on these treadles. Since a thin pick is made in the opposite shed to each thick pick, treadles 9–16 are used for the thin pick and are tied opposite to treadles 1–8 (see *6*, p. 98).

The same process is followed for 8-shaft warp rep with four independent blocks (treadles 1–4 are tied like the profile tie-up for shafts 1–4; shafts 5–8 are tied opposite to shafts 1–4 on treadles 1–4; treadles 5–8 are tied the opposite to treadles 1–4. For four shafts, the profile tie-up is used for shafts 1–2 on treadles 1–2; shafts 3–4 are tied opposite; treadles 3–4 are tied opposite to treadles 1–2.

To weave, follow the squares in the treadling profile draft for the thick pick. For the thin pick, use the opposite treadle (treadle 9 after treadle 1 on 16 shafts; treadle 5 after treadle 1 on eight shafts; treadle 3 after treadle 1 on four). Repeat as necessary to square the block (for Ocean Etude, four thick/thin weft pairs square 48-end blocks).

FOUR BLOCKS ON FOUR SHAFTS

Eight blocks of independent pattern allow many possible designs! If you are limited to a 4-shaft loom, however, the good news is that four blocks of warp rep can be woven on a 4-shaft loom with just one limitation. Blocks must share shafts in the threading. The result is that two blocks always weave pattern or background together (none can make pattern alone nor can more than two make pattern together).

4-shaft, 4-block threading

In this threading, Block A = 1P, 3B; Block B = 2P, 4B; Block C = 3P, 1B; Block D: 4P, 2B; see *1d*.

Two shafts are always raised for the thick pick (either 1-2, 2-3, 3-4, or 4-1) and the opposite two shafts for the thin pick. The pattern color therefore always shows in two blocks at the same time.

This principle of threading pattern ends on the same shafts as background ends and vice versa to gain more blocks can be applied to eight shafts (for eight blocks) and sixteen shafts (for sixteen blocks).

thick 'n thin thick 'n thin

on Rosalie Neilson Rosalie Neilson Rosalie Neilson Rosalie Neilson Rosalie Neilson Rosalie Neilson Rosalie Neilson R

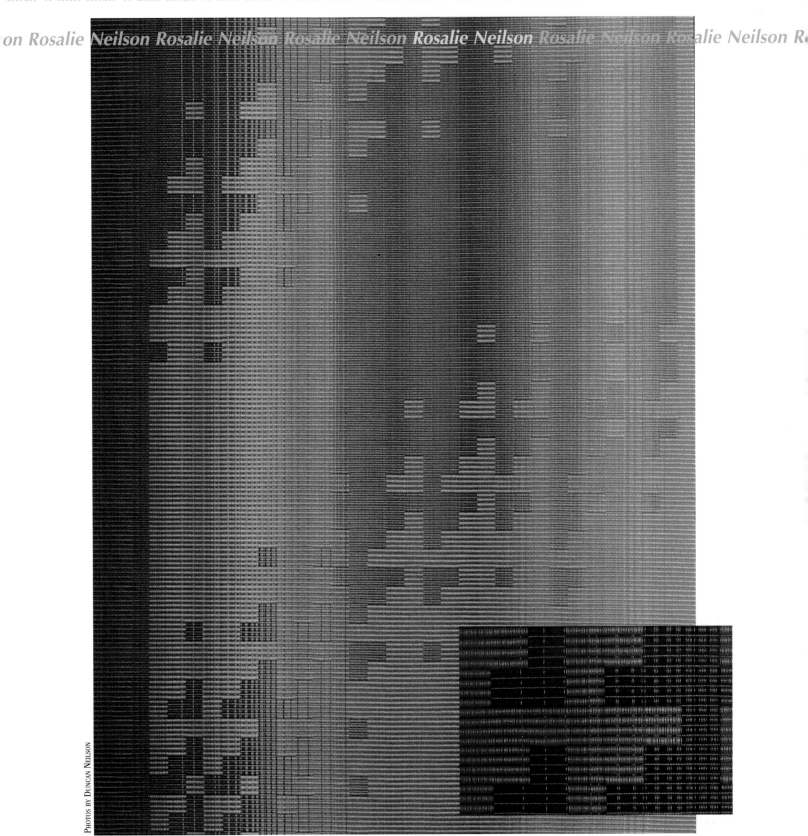

PHOTOS BY DUNCAN NEILSON

In Ocean Etude the pattern warp colorway shades from pale blue on the right to dark blue on the left.
The background warp colorway is a repeated stripe consisting of magentas, pinks, oranges, and reds.

k 'n thin thick 'n thin thick 'n thin thick 'n thin thick 'n thin thick 'n thin thick 'n thin thick 'n thin thick 'n thin thick 'n thin thick 'n thin
thin thick 'n thin thick 'n thin thick 'n thin thick 'n thin thick 'n thin thick 'n thin thick 'n thin thick 'n thin thick 'n thin thick 'n thin thick 'n thin
k 'n thin thick 'n thin thick 'n thin thick 'n thin thick 'n thin thick 'n thin thick 'n thin thick 'n thin thick 'n thin thick 'n thin thick 'n thin

2a. Threading for 4-shaft sampler

first section

A B C D A B C D A D C B A D C B A 1 2 3 4

(threading grid)

3x 3x 3x 3x 3x 3x 3x 3x 3x 3x 3x 3x 3x 3x 3x 3x 3x

second section

A B C B C D C D A D A B A B C B C D

(threading grid)

3x 3x 3x 3x 3x 3x 3x 3x 3x 3x 3x 3x 3x 3x 3x 3x 3x 3x

third section

D A B C B A D C B C D A B C B A D

(threading grid)

3x 3x 3x 3x 3x 3x 3x 3x 3x 3x 3x 3x 3x 3x 3x 3x 3x

2b. Treadling for 4-shaft sampler

Treadle the following pairs (numbers are treadle numbers; first weft is thick, second weft is thin). Alternate treadles 1 and 3 with thin weft for heading and to separate samples. In the instructions for Sample 1, for example, 1-3 4x means to alternate a thick weft with treadle 1 and a thin weft with treadle 3 four times.

Sample 1: 1-3 4x; 2-4 4x; 3-1 4x, 4-2 4x.

Sample 2: 1-3; 2-4; 3-1; 2-4; 3-1; 4-2; 3-1; 4-2; 1-3; 4-2; 1-3; 2-4; 1-3; 2-4; 3-1; 2-4; 3-1; 4-2; 1-3; 2-4; 3-1; 4-2; 3-1; 2-4; 1-3; 4-2; 3-1; 2-4; 3-1; 2-4; 1-3; 2-4; 1-3; 4-2; 1-3; 4-2; 3-1; 4-2; 3-1; 2-4; 3-1; 2-4; 1-3.

Sample 3: Design a: 4-2; 1-3; 2-4; 3-1; 2-4; 1-3; 4-2; 3-1; 2-4; 3-1; 4-2; 1-3; 2-4; 3-1; 2-4; 1-3; 4-2. Design b: 1-3; 2-4; 3-1; 2-4; 3-1; 2-4; 3-1; 4-2; 1-3; 4-2; 1-3; 2-4; 3-1; 2-4; 3-1; 4-2. Design c: 1-3; 2-4; 3-1; 4-2; 1-3; 2-4; 3-1; 4-2; 1-3; 4-2; 3-1; 2-4; 1-3.

4-SHAFT 4-BLOCK SAMPLER

In this sampler, 12 ends (6 pattern, 6 background) are threaded for each square on the profile threading draft in *3*. One thick pick and one thin pick square the block. (For larger-scale projects, use 24 ends for each block—12 pattern and 12 background ends; and two picks each of alternating thick and thin wefts to square a block.)

❏ Equipment. 4-shaft loom, 22–24" weaving width; 10-dent reed; 1 boat shuttle and 2 ski shuttles.

❏ Materials. Warp: 3/2 pearl cotton (1260 yds/lb) in two contrasting colors, a pattern color and a background color, 12 oz pattern color, 14 oz background color. Thick weft: rug filler (75% cotton, 25% rayon, 150 yds/lb, Maysville), 200 yd (1⅓ lb). Thin weft: 3/2 pearl cotton, 3 oz.

❏ Wind a warp 3 yds long (more if loom waste is greater than ½ yd) alternating 1P/1B for 204 ends. Switch to background color only and wind 12 or 24 ends to provide a separation between designs. Switch back to two threads (1P/1B) and wind 216

total ends for second design. Switch to background color only and wind 12 or 24 ends. Switch back to two threads and wind 204 ends for third design. Total number of threads is 648 with a little under ½" between designs or 672 with a little under 1" between designs.

❏ Beam the warp; place lease sticks behind heddles for threading.

❏ Thread following the draft in *2a*. Between the three design sections, thread the background-colored ends 1-3-2-4; repeat to desired width.

❏ Sley 3/dent in a 10-dent reed, 30 epi; center for 21⅗" (with 12-end dividing sections) or 22½" (with 24-end dividing sections).

❏ Wind a bobbin of 3/2 cotton to use for the thin pick. Wind two ski shuttles, each with one strand of rug filler (complete weft is a doubled thread of rug filler) to use for the thick pick.

❏ Weave a ½" heading with the thin weft, raising any opposite pair of shafts. For the designs in *3*, follow the treadling directions in *2b*. Sample 1 defines

the pattern blocks. Sample 2 weaves a point design. In sample 3, the same order is followed for each of the three designs in the treadling as in the threading. For a fourth sample, experiment with your own designs. The only requirement is that after stepping on a treadle for the thick pick, you must step on its opposite for the thin pick.

❏ Weaving tip: First throw the ski shuttle with one strand of thick weft. Beat in place. Keep the shed open and throw the second ski shuttle with the thick weft from the same direction. Beat in place and change to opposite shed. Throw 1 pick thin weft from the same direction and beat. Weave the 2 thick and 1 thin picks in the next sequence from the opposite direction and continue.

❏ To separate the samples, weave ½–1" with thin weft only in opposite sheds.

If the weaving width of your loom is less than 22", thread only one of the designs instead of all three together. The finished weaving width is about 7" for each design.

94

3. Sampler profile draft

Sample 1

Sample 2

Sample 3

8-SHAFT WARP REP

Although four independent blocks of warp rep can be woven on eight shafts (see *1b*, p. 92), *eight* blocks can be woven on eight shafts when blocks weave 'four by four' (similarly to the way four blocks weave 'two by two' on four shafts).

The threading draft

The draft in *4* gives an 8-shaft threading for eight blocks. Notice that the pattern ends (P) for the first four blocks are controlled by shafts 1, 2, 3, 4. In the fifth block, the pattern end is threaded on shaft 5 and the background end on shaft 1 (the reverse of Block A). Therefore, whenever a pattern end in Block A is raised, a background end is raised in Block E. In like manner, shafts 6, 7, and 8 are threaded with pattern ends and 2, 3, 4 with corresponding background ends so that whenever Blocks B, C, or D weave pattern, Blocks F, G, and H weave background and vice versa.

The treadling order: four by four

With this limitation in mind, an 8-block profile threading draft as in *5* can be used for warp rep on eight shafts. Each square in the profile threading represents a designated number of P and B ends, two each in *4*. Note that the profile tie-up shows four blocks producing pattern in each column. Filled-in squares in the profile drawdown represent the pattern-colored warp ends and blank squares the background-colored warp ends raised for the thick picks.

To weave the profile design, first the pattern-colored warp ends are raised for the thick picks (and therefore also the background-colored warp ends threaded on the same shafts). Then the opposite shafts are raised for the thin pick. (Notice that when a block changes from pattern to background or vice versa for a thick pick, the same warp threads are raised as in the preceding thin pick.) The reverse side of the woven fabric shows the opposite colors.

8-SHAFT 8-BLOCK SAMPLER

This sampler is composed of three threading orders and ten treadling sequences for 30 different designs. In the tie-up in *6*, 16 treadles show two different 4/4 twills, one on treadles 1–8, the other on treadles 9–16. Each thick pick is followed by a thin pick in the opposite shed. Opposite treadle pairs are 1-5, 2-6, 3-7, 4-8, 9-13, 10-14, 11-15, 12-16.

- ❑ Equipment. 8-shaft loom, 24" weaving width; 10-dent reed; 1 boat shuttle and 2 ski shuttles.

4. Eight blocks of warp rep weave 'four by four'

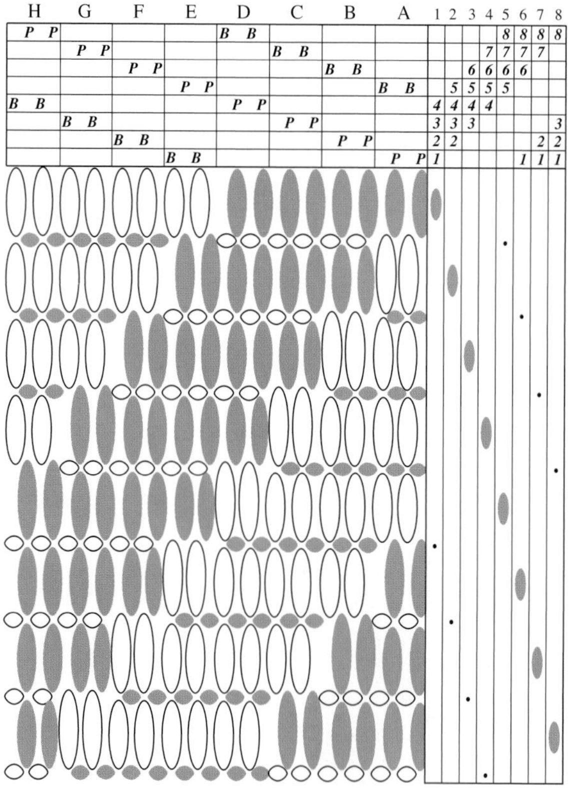
H G F E D C B A 1 2 3 4 5 6 7 8
P P B B 8 8 8 8
P P B B 7 7 7 7
P P B B 6 6 6 6
P P B B 5 5 5 5
B B P P 4 4 4 4
B B P P 3 3 3 3
B B P P 2 2 2 2
B B P P 1 1 1 1

Thread each block 3x (12 ends total each).

- ❑ Materials. Warp: 3/2 pearl cotton (1250 yds/lb) in two contrasting colors, a pattern color (P), 1¼ lb, and a background color (B), 1½ lb. Thin weft: 3/2 pearl cotton, 4 oz. Thick weft: rug filler (75% cotton, 25% rayon, 75 yds/skein, 150 yds/lb, Maysville), 5 lbs.
- ❑ Wind a warp 4½ yds long alternating 1 P/1B, 180 total ends for first design. Switch to background color and wind 12 or 24 ends to separate designs. Switch back to 1P/1B for 192 ends for second design. Switch to background color only and wind 12 or 24 ends. Switch back 1P/1B for 252 ends for third design (648 or 672 total ends).
- ❑ Beam the warp.
- ❑ Thread by substituting the threading for each block (3x) in *4* for each square in the profile threading in *8*. Thread the separating sections on any block, such as Block A (alternate 1, 5).
- ❑ Sley 3/dent in a 10-dent reed for 30 epi; center for 21⅗" or 22⅜".
- ❑ Tie up treadles as in *6*. For looms with limited treadles, tie up the first eight treadles for samples 1–3. Retie for 4–6. For 7, retie in the middle of the treadling sequence. If you do not have 16 treadles for samples 8–10, try designing a new tie-up and use the treadling orders for samples 1–3.
- ❑ Weave a 2" heading for hem with thin weft, alternating treadles 1 and 5. Weave the samples; end with 2" heading.

5. Sample 8-block profile

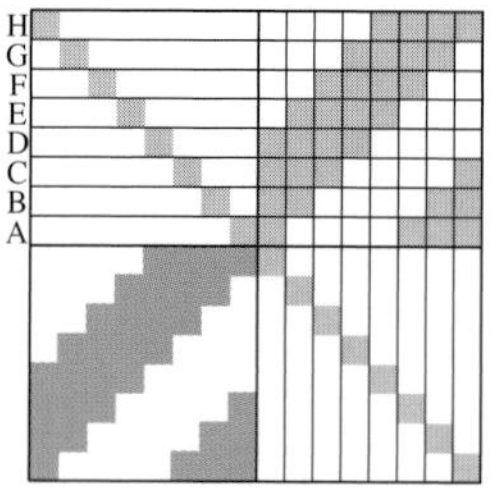
H
G
F
E
D
C
B
A

6. Tie-up for sampler

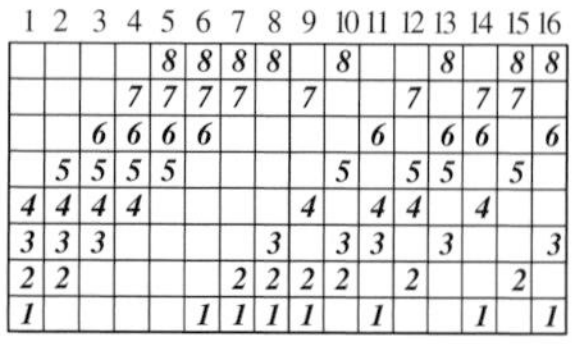
1 2 3 4 5 6 7 8 9 10 11 12 13 14 15 16

7. Treadling for sampler

Instructions indicate treadle pairs: use left treadle for thick pick, right treadle for thin pick. Separate each design by weaving with thin weft only, using treadles 1 and 5 five times.

1
1-5, 2-6, 3-7, 4-8, 5-1, 6-2, 7-3, 8-4, 7-3, 6-2, 5-1, 4-8, 3-7, 2-6, 1-5

2
1-5, 4-8, 7-3, 2-6, 5-1, 8-4, 3-7, 6-2, 1-5, 4-8, 7-3, 2-6, 5-1, 8-4, 3-7, 6-2

3
1-5, 2-6, 3-7, 2-6, 3-7, 4-8, 3-7, 4-8, 5-1, 4-8, 5-1, 6-2, 5-1, 6-2, 7-3, 6-2, 7-3, 8-4, 7-3, 8-4, 1-5

4
9-13, 10-14, 11-15, 12-16, 13-9, 14-10, 15-11, 16-12, 15-11, 14-10, 13-9, 12-16, 11-15, 10-14, 9-13

5
9-13, 12-16, 15-11, 10-14, 13-9, 16-12, 11-15, 14-10, 9-13, 12-16, 15-11, 10-14, 13-9, 16-12, 11-15, 14-10

6
9-13, 10-14, 11-15, 10-14, 11-15, 12-16, 11-15, 12-16, 13-9, 12-16, 13-9, 14-10, 13-9, 14-10, 15-11, 14-10, 15-11, 16-12, 15-11, 16-12, 9-13

7
1-5, 2-6, 3-7, 4-8, 5-1, 6-2, 7-3, 8-4, 9-13, 10-14, 11-15, 12-16, 13-9, 14-10, 15-11, 16-12, *reverse*

8
16-12, 8-4, 15-11, 7-3, 14-10, 6-2, 13-9, 5-1, 12-16, 4-8, 11-15, 3-7, 10-4, 2-6, 9-13, *reverse*

9
1-5, 9-13, 4-8, 12-16, 7-3, 15-11, 2-6, 10-14, 5-1, 13-9, 8-4, 16-12, 3-7, 11-15, 6-2, 14-10

10
4-8, 3-7, 13-9, 10-14, 2-6, 12-16, 15-11, 7-3, 9-13, 1-5, 8-4, 16-12, 11-15, 14-10, 6-2, *reverse*

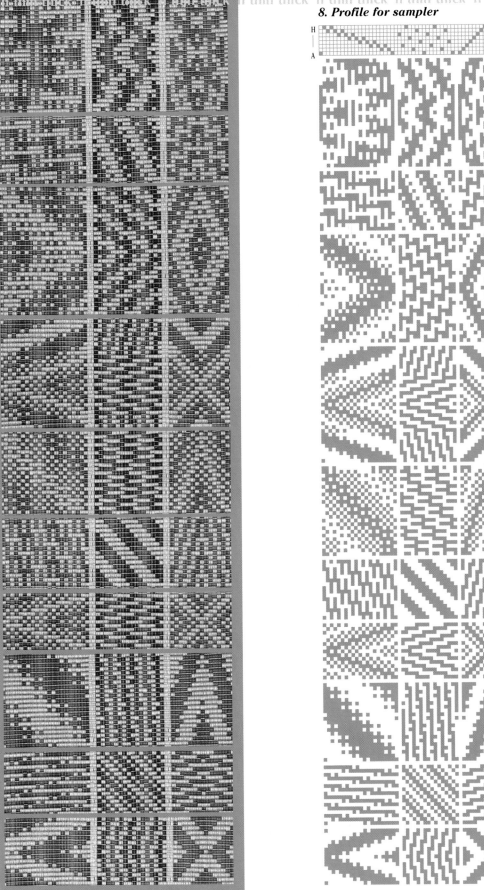

8. Profile for sampler

ck 'n thin thick 'n thin thick 'n thin thick 'n thin thick 'n thin thick 'n thin thick 'n thin thick 'n thin thick 'n thin thick 'n thin thick 'n thic
ck 'n thin thick 'n thin thick 'n thin thick 'n thin thick 'n thin thick 'n thin thick 'n thin thick 'n thin thick 'n thin thick 'n thin thick 'n thin thic
thin thick 'n thin thick 'n thin thick 'n thin thick 'n thin thick 'n thin thick 'n thin thick 'n thin thick 'n thin thick 'n thin thick 'n thin thick 'n
'n thin thick 'n thin thick 'n thin thick 'n thin thick 'n thin thick 'n thin thick 'n thin thick 'n thin thick 'n thin thick 'n thin thick 'n thin thic

SIXTEEN BLOCKS ON SIXTEEN SHAFTS

Examine the draft in *9*. Eight pairs of blocks are interconnected by the shafts they share. Where one shaft of one pair carries the pattern color, the same shaft in the other pair carries the background color: A and I share shafts 1 and 9, B and J shafts 2 and 10, C and K shafts 3 and 11, D and L shafts 4 and 12, E and M shafts 5 and 13, F and N shafts 6 and 14, G and O shafts 7 and 15, H and P shafts 8 and 16.

Eight by eight

Each square in the 16-block profile threading draft in *10* is interpreted as two P/B pairs in the warp rep draft in *9*. The profile tie-up in *10* shows eight blocks combined in each vertical column. In the profile drawdown in *10*, filled-in squares represent the pattern-colored warp ends; blank squares represent the background-colored warp ends. Each square in the treadling draft is interpreted as two picks of weft in *9*, a thick pick using one combination of eight shafts, followed by a thin pick with the opposite eight. Remember that each time eight pattern shafts are raised, eight background shafts also come along for the ride.

Designing 16-block warp rep tie-ups working from quadrants

There are several ways to derive tie-ups for weaving warp rep that observe the 'eight by eight' limitation. On graph paper, draw a box surrounding 16 columns and 16 rows. The columns represent blocks A–P (and shafts 1–16). Next divide the box into 8 x 8-square quadrants. Quadrant 1 controls the colors of block A–H; quadrant 2 controls the colors of blocks I–P; quadrants 3 and 4 represent the opposite-colored blocks for I–P and A–H respectively (for the opposite, thin picks).

With a pencil, blacken a square or series of squares in the first quadrant to represent the pattern-colored blocks. Blank squares represent the background-colored blocks. The color of blocks A–H (pattern or background) have now been determined in quadrant 1. Since blocks share the same pair of shafts, the second set of blocks in quadrant 2 are filled in opposite to quadrant 1. For example, blocks A and I share shafts 1 and 9. If block A is filled in, block I is left blank.

Since two picks of weft are used in warp rep, a thick pick in one shed followed by a thin pick in the opposite shed, quadrants 3 and 4 are used to develop the opposite sheds for the thin picks. The block colors in quadrant 3 are opposite to those of quadrant 2; and in quadrant 4 opposite to those of quadrant 1.

Any 8-shaft twill tie-up can be used as a basis for quadrant 1. For example, using a 3/5 twill, darken the first three squares in quadrant 1 (A, B, C) and leave the next five blank (D, E, F, G, H). In quadrant 2, leave the first three squares blank (I, J, K) and darken the last five (L, M, N, O, P). Quadrant 3 shows the reverse colors of quadrant 2; quadrant 4 shows the reverse colors of quadrant 1.

The four quadrants form the 16-shaft 16-treadle tie-up in *11*. If the first treadle on the left is used for a thick pick, pattern is formed in A, B, C, L, M, N, O, P. The 9th treadle shows the opposite lift and is used for the corresponding thin pick.

Deriving 16-block warp rep tie-ups from 16-shaft twills

Any 16-shaft twill with equal portions of filled-in and blank squares (corresponding to eight pattern and eight background blocks) can be used for 16-block warp rep. For a 3/1/2/5/1/2/2 twill, for example, darken squares in the first column of a 16 x 16 square grid: 3 black, 1 white, 2 black, 5 white, 1 black, 2 white, 2 black. Step up one square in each successive column. If this twill is separated into four quadrants, it follows the rule as above: quadrants 1 and 4 are opposites for blocks A-H, and quadrants 2 and 3 are opposites for blocks I-P.

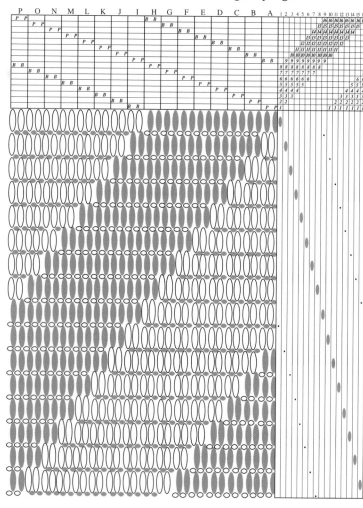

9. Sixteen blocks of warp rep weave `eight by eight'

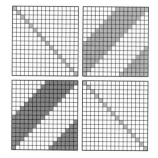

10. Profile draft for 9

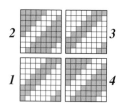

11. Tie-up derived from an 8-shaft 3/5 twill

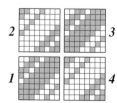

12a. 16-shaft 8/8 twill tie-up

12b. Tie-up 12a showing quadrant opposites

'n thin thick 'n thin thick 'n thin thick 'n thin thick 'n thin thick 'n thin thick 'n thin thick 'n thin thick 'n thin thick 'n thin thick 'n thin thick '
thin thick 'n thin thick 'n thin thick 'n thin thick 'n thin thick 'n thin thick 'n thin thick 'n thin thick 'n thin thick 'n thin thick 'n thin thick 'n
k 'n thin thick 'n thin thick 'n thin thick 'n thin thick 'n thin thick 'n thin thick 'n thin thick 'n thin thick 'n thin thick 'n thin thick 'n thin thick
thick 'n thin thick 'n thin thick 'n thin thick 'n thin thick 'n thin thick 'n thin thick 'n thin thick 'n thin thick 'n thin thick 'n thin thick 'n thin
thick 'n thin thick 'n thin thick 'n thin thick 'n thin thick 'n thin thick 'n thin thick 'n thin thick 'n thin thick 'n thin thick 'n thin thick 'n thin t

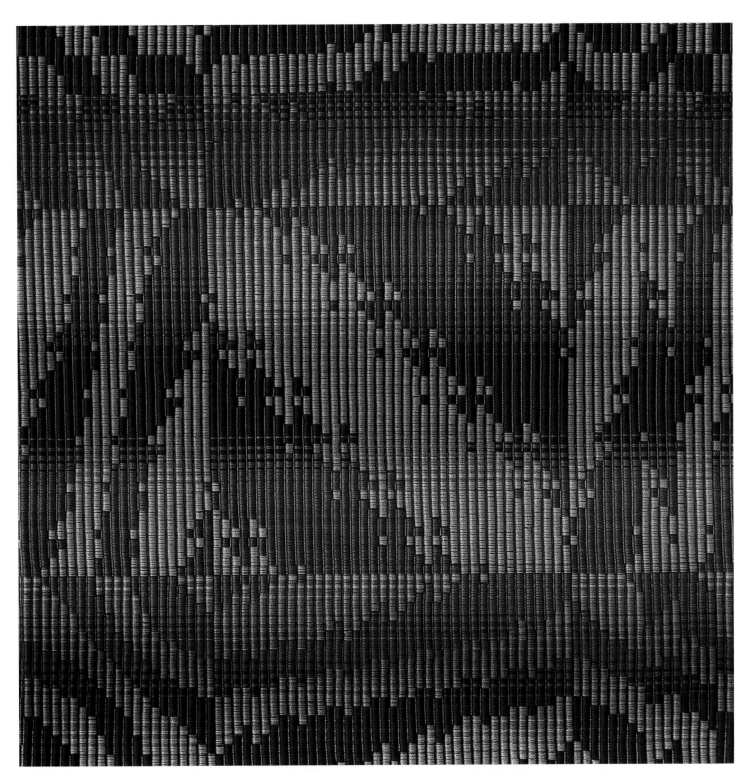

Three different designs in the threading and three different treadling orders of the blocks create this sampler on 16 shafts.
The pattern colorway is in several different shades of red, and the background colorway moves from gold to green to blue.

k 'n thin thick 'n thin thick 'n thin thick 'n thin thick 'n thin thick 'n thin thick 'n thin thick 'n thin thick 'n thin thick 'n thin
k 'n thin thick 'n thin thick 'n thin thick 'n thin thick 'n thin thick 'n thin thick 'n thin thick 'n thin thick 'n thin thick 'n thin
thin thick 'n thin, thick 'n thin, thick 'n thin, thick 'n thin, thick 'n thin, thick & thin, thick 'n thin, thick 'n thin, thick 'n
k 'n thin thick 'n thin thick 'n thin thick 'n thin thick 'n thin thick 'n thin thick 'n thin thick 'n thin thick 'n thin thick

16-SHAFT 16-BLOCK SAMPLER

This last sampler is a free-form design divided into three threading sections and three treadling sequences to yield nine different designs, see photo p. 99. The 16 treadles are arranged in a twill sequence. As with the other samplers, a thick pick (two thicknesses of rug filler) is followed by a thin pick in the opposite shed.

❏ Equipment. 16-shaft loom, 36" weaving width (if weaving all three designs); 10-dent reed; 1 boat shuttle and 2 ski shuttles.

❏ Materials. Warp: 3/2 pearl cotton (1260 yds/lb) in two contrasting colorways, a pattern colorway (P) and a background colorway (B), 1½ lbs each color for all three designs. (In this sampler the pattern colorway is a series of different shades of red, and the background colorway moves through three shades of gold, three shades of green, and three shades of blue.) Thin weft: 3/2 pearl cotton, ¼ lb. Thick weft: rug filler (100% cotton, 75 yds/skein, 150 yds/lb, Maysville), 3 lbs total (two strands are used for each thick pick wound separately on two ski shuttles).

❏ Wind a warp of 960 total ends 3½ yds long using one end pattern color and one end background color (480 ends each color) for all three designs. (If weaving the first design section only, wind 252 ends; second design section only, wind 468 ends; third design section only, wind 240 ends.)

❏ Beam the warp; place lease sticks behind heddles for threading.

❏ Thread by substituting six pattern and six background-colored threads for each square on the profile threading draft, always in P, B, P, B order on the appropriate pairs of shafts. Block A = shafts 1, 9; B = 2, 10; C = 3, 11; D = 4, 12; E = 5, 13; F = 6, 14; G = 7, 15; H = 8, 16; I = 9, 1; J = 10, 2; K = 11, 3; L = 12, 4; M = 13, 5; N = 14, 6; O = 15, 7; P = 16, 8. The complete draft for the center design in *14* is given in *13*.

❏ Sley 3/dent in a 10-dent reed, 30 epi; center for 32" if weaving all three designs.

❏ Tie up the treadles as shown in *13*. (Note that the profile tie-up in *14* is the same as the actual tie-up and that it follows the quadrant rules.) Re-tie treadles as needed for experimentation with other design ideas; this sampler allows about 100" of woven cloth. Twill tie-ups are only one source for designing. The only design limitation is that blocks must weave 'eight by eight.'

13. Draft for the center design in the sampler

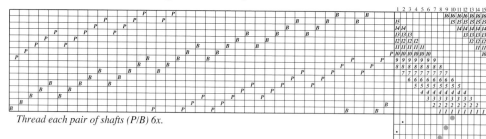

Thread each pair of shafts (P/B) 6x.

14. Profile draft for sampler

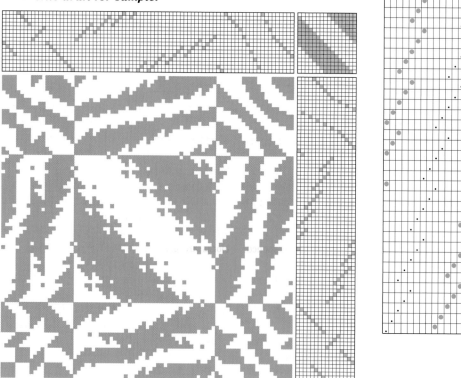

❏ Weave a 2" heading with the thin weft for a hem, alternating treadles 1 and 9. The treadling for the designs in this sampler is 'as-drawn-in'; that is, the numbers of the shafts in the threading are used as the treadle numbers for weaving, except that only 2 picks (1 thick, 1 thin) are used for each treadled block. In *13*, the complete treadling is shown for the center design.

To weave the designs, wind the two ski shuttles with rug filler. Throw the first ski shuttle with the thick weft. Beat in place. Keep the shed open and throw the second ski shuttle with thick weft in the same direction as the first. Beat in place and change to the opposite shed. Throw one pick thin weft, again in the same direction as the thick weft, and beat. Begin the next sequence with all three shuttles moving in the opposite direction.

❏ End with a 2" heading, remove fabric from the loom, turn under headings, and hem.

The samplers shown here on four, eight, and sixteen shafts are only starting points for learning about designing with warp rep. Add to warp length and weave a set of placemats for samplers you can use. You'll soon find yourself ripped about rep! ✄

warp- and weft-faced lampas

sy Blumenthal *Betsy Blumenthal* *Betsy Blumenthal* **Betsy Blumenthal** *Betsy Blumenthal* *Betsy Blumentl*

"This weave structure is the most successful solution so far in my search for a double weave with both a warp-faced layer and a weft-faced layer. I have tried adapting traditional multishaft double weave with its independent exchanging layers to this end, but the resulting fabric lacks structural unity since the layers are connected only at the edge of each pattern block. In addition, because pattern blocks require four shafts each in the usual form of double weave, complex patterns in it are beyond the capacity of most looms."

By contrast, the following weave structure (which might be called a 'plain weave integrated lampas') is a completely integrated textile in which an almost invisible weft thread connects the two layers at regular intervals. The fabric is structurally reversible: the warp-faced areas on the front side are weft-faced on the reverse and vice versa.

A LAMPAS VARIATION

Lampas is a double weave in which a stable 50/50 main or foundation weave (plain weave, twill, or satin) is patterned with a secondary weave that consists of a very fine warp and a heavy weft. To produce this lampas variation, instead of a 50/50 balanced weave, the main weave is formed by a thick warp closely sett to become a warp-faced structure as it weaves with a fine weft.

The threading

Pattern blocks in lampas are determined by the threading of the the main weave. Each block requires the number of shafts that produce the selected structure, two for plain weave, four for 4-thread twill, etc.

The fine warp that weaves with the heavy weft to form the weft-faced secondary weave is threaded on a single set of shafts just as it is in a standard lampas (two for plain weave, four for 4-thread twill, five for 5-thread satin, etc.; see the draft in *1*).

The treadling

For this variation, the standard lampas treadling sequence is altered so that either three or four picks of the heavy (secondary) weft are woven and packed tightly together after each fine (main) weave pick. In this way, the 'main' weave and the 'secondary' weave

Warp-faced and weft-faced lampas; the ratio of thick to thin is 4:1.

are structurally identical and neither is subordinate to the other—the fine weft of the main weave interlaces with the thick warp just as the fine warp of the secondary weave interlaces with the thick weft.

Loom requirements

In this plain weave/plain weave variation of lampas two shafts are required for the secondary (weft-faced) weave and two additional shafts for each pattern block of the warp-faced main weave; three blocks are possible on eight shafts, five blocks on 12 shafts, seven blocks on 16 shafts, etc. The two warps (the heavy main warp and the fine secondary warp) require two back beams so that equal tension can be maintained. The fine warp is threaded on the back shafts in this version so that the thick warp is as close to the front of the loom as possible to aid in clearing the potentially sticky sheds (see *1*).

Further notes

I have tried two versions of the threading: one with a ratio of three main weave (thick) ends to each secondary (thin) end and the other with four to one (see *1*). The project sampler uses the 4:1 version. The ratio of thick picks to thin picks for each of these threadings corresponds to the threading ratio: when three thick ends are threaded for each thin end, three thick picks are woven for each thin pick; when four thick ends are threaded between thin warp ends, four thick wefts are woven between thin picks. These treadling sequences may produce blocks that are somewhat taller than square, depending on the materials and the sett used. Sample to determine the

most successful materials and numbers of picks.

The thick yarns must be somewhat soft so as to expand to cover the thin threads, yet not so soft and sticky as to interfere with the formation of a clear shed in the closely sett warp-faced sections. I keep a pick-up stick handy to clear the shed when necessary. Wool yarns with a relatively firm, smooth finish prove a very suitable choice for thick warp and weft. I have also used a 2-ply silk noil for the thick yarn. The yarn used for the fine warp and weft should be strong and firmly plied and about one quarter the size of the thick yarn. A cotton or cotton/linen blend in a color that matches or is a little darker than the thick yarns works well for the thin yarns.

GETTING STARTED

The sampler suggested here uses Harrisville Designs 2-ply wool for the thick warp and weft and 22/2 cotton/linen blend for the thin warp and weft (8/4 cotton carpet warp would work as well). The resulting textile is thick and firm.

Eight shafts are used for three blocks threaded in bird's-eye twill order. For simplicity's sake all of the threading blocks in the sample are the same size. Of course, as with any unit weave, blocks can be threaded and woven in any order and size. The sample uses only three of many possible combinations and treadling orders of the three blocks. Select any three-block profile draft, or translate any 3-end twill into a profile draft for design variation.

To illustrate how color-and-weave patterns can be incorporated into the warp- and weft-faced areas, the thick warp in this sampler is threaded one-and-one with two close colors; weft stripes can be created by alternating two colors in the thick weft.

1. Threading units for thick 'n thin lampas

4:1 ratio of thick ends to thin ends

3:1 ratio of thick ends to thin ends

2. Draft for sampler

tie-up a

tie-up b

1	2	3	4	5	6	7	8
8		8		8		8	
7		7		7		7	
			6	6		6	
			5	5		5	
	4	4					4
	3	3					3
2	2	2	2	2			2
1	1	1	1	1	1		

tie-up c

1	2	3	4	5	6
8		8		8	
7		7		7	
6	6				6
5	5			5	
4	4				4
3	3		3		
2	2	2	2		2
1	1	1	1	1	

WARP- AND WEFT-FACED LAMPAS SAMPLER

This sampler is only the beginning of an exploration of this weave. See also Betsy's pillows, pp 104–105. If more than eight shafts are available, thread the blocks in a point or choose another arrangement to experiment with design. The primary advantage of this weave is that pure undiluted warp colors contrast with pure undiluted weft colors. Try finer smoother fibers for the thick threads in closer setts for upholstery or clothing.

Because this structure requires two beams (or separate tensions for the two warps), use the method of warping for two beams that you are accustomed to or that is appropriate for your equipment. If you decide to weight one of the warps and beam the other, choose the fine warp to suspend and weight, but you may have some difficulty keeping tension even and firm on these threads. The thick warp requires a beam, since it is likely to be sticky and will only be manageable if the tension is absolutely even throughout.

❑ Equipment. 8-shaft loom, 22" weaving width, 2 back beams if available; 10-dent reed; 1 boat shuttle and 2 stick shuttles.

❑ Materials. Thick warp: 2-ply wool (1000 yds/lb, Harrisville), Charcoal 5 oz, Purple Haze 5 oz. Thick weft: 2-ply wool, Purple Haze 2 oz, Peacock 2 oz, Cobalt 2 oz, Sage (tweed) 2 oz, Clay (tweed) 2 oz. Thin warp and weft: cottolin (50% cotton/50% linen, 2900 yds/lb), black 2 oz, (or 8/4 carpet warp, black, 4 oz.

❑ Wind the thick warp alternating one end Charcoal and one end Purple Haze, 102 ends each color, 204 total ends, 3 yds long. Wind the thin warp of 51 ends black Cottolin (or carpet warp) 3 yds long.

❑ Sley 2 thick ends (one of each color) in each dent of a 10-dent reed (for 20 epi) and one thin end in every other dent (for 5 epi).

❑ Thread substituting threading units in *2* for the corresponding squares on the profile

draft in *3* so that Purple Haze is always threaded on odd shafts, Charcoal on even shafts. Add 2 floating selvedges to each side, one in each of the two warp colors.

❑ Beam the two warps separately or beam the thick warp and suspend the thin warp from the back beam in small chains and weight.

❑ Weave a plain weave heading and sections between samples with the thin black weft. Weave the designs by substituting the treadling sequences in *2* for squares on the treadling profile drafts in *3*. Weave the first two samples using tie-up *a* and profile treadling *a*. For one, use Peacock pattern weft. For the other, alternate Cobalt and Peacock 1/1 to produce vertical stripes. Next use use tie-up *b* and profile treadling *b* with Sage pattern weft. Then use tie-up *c* and profile treadling *c* with Clay pattern weft. Finally, use tie-up *a* and profile treadling *a* and alternate Sage and Purple Haze 2/2 to produce horizontal stripes. After completing these five sampler sequences, experiment by changing block and color orders.

❑ Hints. Use a pick-up stick just in front of the reed to help clear the shed if sticky. For a neat, closely packed thick weft, when you weave the thin weft, turn the pick-up stick on its side and bring it firmly forward to the last row of weaving before inserting the next thick weft.

❑ For further study, use this structure in soft materials for blankets and in heavy, firm wools for rugs and upholstery. ✂

3. Sampler profile drafts

use with tie-up a

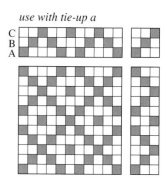

use with tie-up b

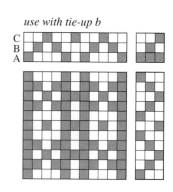

use with tie-up c

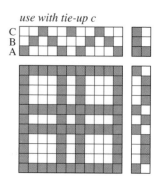

thin thick 'n thin thick 'n thin thick 'n thin thick 'n thin thick 'n thin thick 'n thin thick 'n thin thick 'n thin thick 'n thin thick 'n thin thick 'n thin thick
thin thick 'n thin thick 'n thin thick 'n thin thick 'n thin thick 'n thin thick 'n thin thick 'n thin thick 'n thin thick 'n thin thick 'n
thick 'n thin thick 'n thin thick 'n thin thick 'n thin thick 'n thin thick 'n thin thick 'n thin thick 'n thin thick 'n thin thick 'n thin thick
thick 'n thin thick 'n thin thick 'n thin thick 'n thin thick 'n thin thick 'n thin thick 'n thin thick 'n thin thick 'n thin t

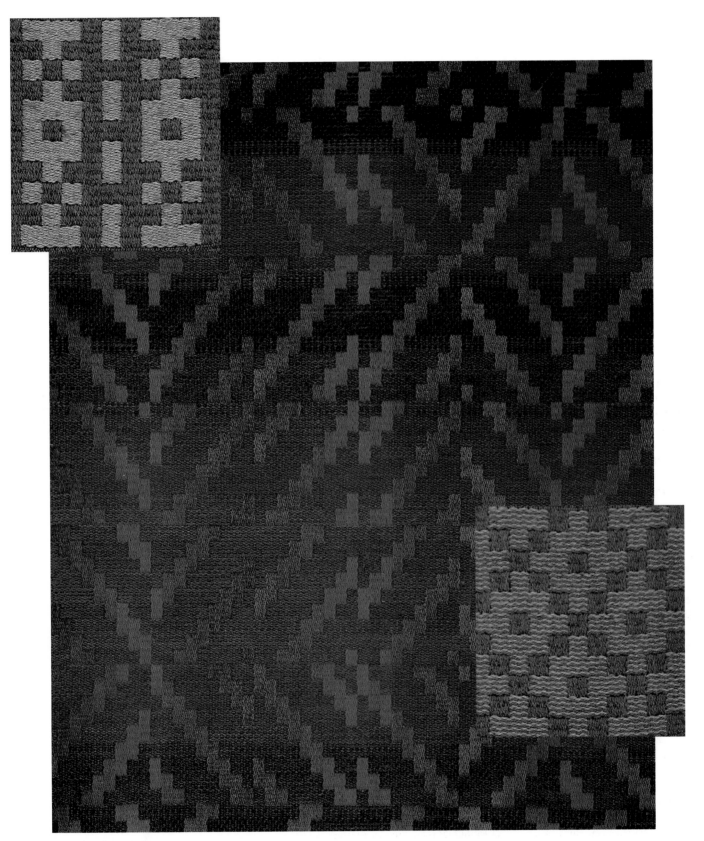

The lampas variation in Twill Imagery provides solid-color contrast between warp-faced and weft-faced areas. Practice with a sampler (inset at top left uses tie-up b; inset at bottom right uses tie-up a).

networked thick 'n thin lampas pillows

Betsy Blumenthal *Betsy Blumenthal Betsy Blumenthal Betsy Blumenthal* **Betsy Blumenthal** *Betsy Blumenthal Betsy Blume*

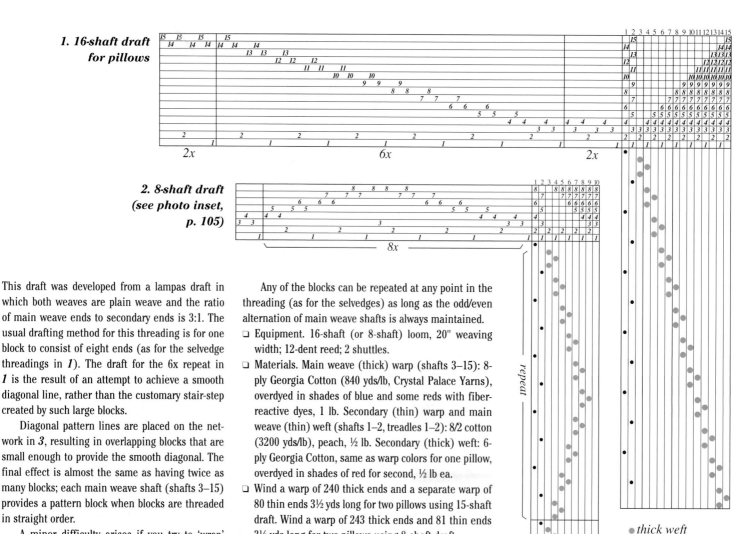

1. 16-shaft draft for pillows

2. 8-shaft draft (see photo inset, p. 105)

• thick weft
• thin weft

This draft was developed from a lampas draft in which both weaves are plain weave and the ratio of main weave ends to secondary ends is 3:1. The usual drafting method for this threading is for one block to consist of eight ends (as for the selvedge threadings in *1*). The draft for the 6x repeat in *1* is the result of an attempt to achieve a smooth diagonal line, rather than the customary stair-step created by such large blocks.

Diagonal pattern lines are placed on the network in *3*, resulting in overlapping blocks that are small enough to provide the smooth diagonal. The final effect is almost the same as having twice as many blocks; each main weave shaft (shafts 3–15) provides a pattern block when blocks are threaded in straight order.

A minor difficulty arises if you try to 'wrap' a half block from the last shaft back to shaft 3: a long float develops. (Such a float appears on the back of the fabric produced by the 8-shaft draft.) In addition, an even number of blocks is necessary to ensure that both main and secondary weaves repeat on the same cycle.

In another break from the usual lampas threading, for this fabric thick threads are used for the main warp ends to give a warp-faced main weave (contrasting strongly with the weft-faced secondary weave).

Any of the blocks can be repeated at any point in the threading (as for the selvedges) as long as the odd/even alternation of main weave shafts is always maintained.

❑ Equipment. 16-shaft (or 8-shaft) loom, 20" weaving width; 12-dent reed; 2 shuttles.
❑ Materials. Main weave (thick) warp (shafts 3–15): 8-ply Georgia Cotton (840 yds/lb, Crystal Palace Yarns), overdyed in shades of blue and some reds with fiber-reactive dyes, 1 lb. Secondary (thin) warp and main weave (thin) weft (shafts 1–2, treadles 1–2): 8/2 cotton (3200 yds/lb), peach, ½ lb. Secondary (thick) weft: 6-ply Georgia Cotton, same as warp colors for one pillow, overdyed in shades of red for second, ½ lb ea.
❑ Wind a warp of 240 thick ends and a separate warp of 80 thin ends 3½ yds long for two pillows using 15-shaft draft. Wind a warp of 243 thick ends and 81 thin ends 3½ yds long for two pillows using 8-shaft draft.
❑ Sley 1 thick end/dent and 1 thin end every 3rd dent (1-0-0-1-0-0, etc.) for 12 epi thick warp and 4 epi thin warp; center for 20" 15-shaft draft, 20¼" 8-shaft draft.
❑ Thread as in *1* for 15-shaft draft, *2* for 8-shaft draft.
❑ Weave following treadling in *1* or *2* for two pillow faces with backs. For a seam allowance, begin and end each pillow with 1" thin weft using only treadles 1 and 2.
❑ Finish by cutting apart the pillows; fold right sides together for each, stitch side seams together; stuff; turn and sew last edge by hand. ✄

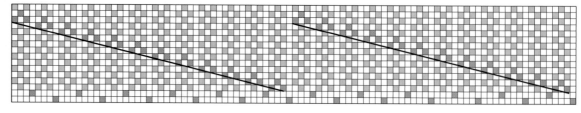

3. Pattern line is placed on lampas network to derive the threading in 1

thin thick 'n thin thick 'n thin thick 'n thin thick 'n thin thick 'n thin thick 'n thin thick 'n thin thick 'n thin thick 'n thin thick 'n thin thick 'n thin thick 'n thin thick 'n thin thick 'n t
'n thin thick 'n thin thick 'n thin thick 'n thin thick 'n thin thick 'n thin thick 'n thin thick 'n thin thick 'n thin thick 'n thin thick 'n thin thick
thick 'n thin thick 'n thin thick 'n thin thick 'n thin thick 'n thin thick 'n thin thick 'n thin thick 'n thin thick 'n thin th

8-shaft networked lampas

Weave these quick and easy networked lampas pillows on sixteen shafts or the diamond design on eight (see inset above). You'll enjoy the texture and visual excitement of watching the pattern grow.

thick 'n thin thick 'n thin thick 'n thin thick 'n thin thick 'n thin thick 'n thin thick 'n thin thick 'n thin thick 'n thin thick
'n thin thick 'n thin thick 'n thin thick 'n thin thick 'n thin thick 'n thin thick 'n thin thick 'n thin thick 'n thin thick 'n thin thick
thin thick 'n thin thick 'n thin thick 'n thin thick 'n thin thick 'n thin thick 'n thin thick 'n thin thick 'n thin thick 'n thin thick 'n
'n thin thick 'n thin thick 'n thin thick 'n thin thick 'n thin thick 'n thin thick 'n thin thick 'n thin thick 'n thin thick 'n thin thick

yarn list

50/3 cotton sewing thread
14,000 yds/lb; 40, 48, 60

30/2 cotton, 12,600 yds/lb
40, 48, 56

20/2 cotton, 8,400 yds/lb
30, 36, 48

16/2 cotton, 6,400 yds/lb
24, 30, 36

10/2 cotton, 4,200 yds/lb
20, 24, 28

8/2 cotton, 3,200 yds/lb
16, 20, 24

cotton slub, 3,000 yds/lb
15, 20, 24

5/2 cotton, 2,100 yds/lb
12, 16, 18

8/4 soft cotton, 1,680 yds/lb
10, 12, 15

8/4 cotton (carpet warp),
1,600 yds/lb; 12, 15, 18

3/2 pearl cotton, 1,260 yds/lb
10, 14, 18

Cotton Classic, 980 yds/lb
8, 10, 12

cotton chenille, 895 yds/lb
8, 10, 12

4/4 cotton Mo-Purl, 840 yds/lb
4, 6, 8

8-ply Georgia cotton, 840 yds/lb
4, 6, 8

Maysville rug filler, 75% cotton,
25% rayon, 150 yds/lb

22/2 cottolin (50% cotton,
50% linen), 3,000 yds/lb; 15, 20, 24

120/2 silk, 40,000 yds/lb
48, 54, 72

30/2 silk, 7,850 yds/lb
24, 32, 40

#4 medium singles silk, 950 yds/lb
8, 10, 12

2-ply softspun silk, 800 yds/lb
8, 10, 12

30/2 wool, 8,400 yds/lb
24, 30, 36

20/2 wool, 5,600 yds/lb
20, 24, 30

18/2 wool/silk, 5,040 yds/lb
20, 24, 30

8/2 wool, 2,240 yds/lb
12, 15, 20

2-ply Shetland wool, 2,000 yds/lb
12, 15, 20

7/2 wool, 1,700 yds/lb
12, 15, 20

Victorian 2-ply wool, 1,475 yds/lb
10, 12, 15

8/4 wool, 1,120 yds/lb
8, 10, 12

2-ply wool, 1,000 yds/lb
8, 10, 12

3-ply rug wool, 400 yds/lb
4, 6, 8

2-ply wool, 392 yds/lb
4, 6, 8

3-ply rug wool, 260 yds/lb
4, 5, 6

rayon sewing thread, 14,240 yds/lb
(890 yds/oz); 30, 40, 48

rayon chenille, 1,450 yds/lb
12, 15, 18

rayon ribbon (Glacé), 75 yds/1.75 oz
6, 8, 10

nylon ribbon (Skacel)
6, 8, 10

other publications from **XRX**

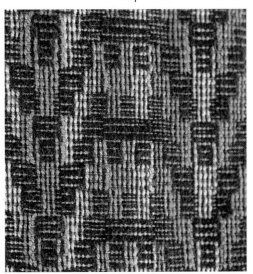

Two Sweaters For My Father
   by Perri Klass

Module Magic

Maggie's Ireland

Jean Frost Jackets

The Knitting Experience:
   The Knit Stitch
   The Purl Stitch

A Knitter's Dozen:
   Angels
   Ponchos and Wraps
   Bags

The Best of Lopi

Best of Weaver's to come: Handpaint Country

Double weave   Gathering of Lace

Overshot   Sculptured Knits

Summer and Winter and Beyond   Sally Melville Styles

Rugs and Weft-faced Weaves   Magnificent Mittens

Finnweave   Ethnic Socks and Stockings

Piqué   Afghans:
   The Great American Afghan
and more   The Great North American Afghan
   The Great American Kid's Afghan
   The Great American Aran Afghan

Socks Socks Socks

Kids Kids Kids

For more information: The Best of Knitter's
www.knittinguniverse.com   Shawls and Scarves
1-800-232-5648   Arans & Celtics

The Best of Weaver's:
   Huck Lace
   Fabrics that go Bump
   Twill Thrills

The Knitter's Handbook

Knitter's Magazine

 BOOKS